People

YEARBOOK

2014!

Contents

14

89

20

62

2013 News

From Prince William's nappy know-how to Kate's 'Mummy Tummy' (and subsequent slimdown) to their nurturing nanny, the Duke and Duchess of Cambridge rewrote the rules of royal parenting

BABY LOVE!

From the moment His Royal Highness Prince George Alexander Louis of Cambridge arrived at 4:24 p.m. on July 22, his parents signaled their intention to forge a path that is both respectful of tradition and "totally modern," a friend told People. For William, that meant breaking with precedent and being by his wife's side starting with their arrival from

Kensington Palace at 6 a.m. and lasting through the night at St. Mary's hospital. But just as William's mother, Princess Diana, did 31 years earlier, clad in a similarly polka-dotted frock on the very same hospital steps, Kate—less than 24 hours after giving birth—gamely introduced her newborn to cheering crowds. "It's very emotional," she told reporters. "It's such a special time. I think any parent will know what this feeling feels like." As the proud prince carefully cradled his securely swaddled son, he added, "He has got her looks, thankfully."

Those looks were, as always, scrutinized. Thanks to a diaphanous Jenny Packham dress that in no way hid her not-yet-washboard abs (those would be on display within three months at a volleyball game), Kate's "mummy tummy" quickly became a viral meme. "She wanted people to see she's real," said Siobhan Freegard of British parenting site Netmums. "That was a lovely message to every mom out there."

Another down-to-earth choice? Spending their first weeks with George at the Bucklebury estate of Kate's parents instead of in the servant-rich confines of Kensington Palace. Such a move would have been unthinkable for a future monarch just one generation ago— but then again, so was the idea of a prince changing diapers (as William does). "I thought Search and Rescue duties over Snowdonia were physically and mentally demanding," he told a farm festival crowd on Aug. 14, "but looking after a 3-week-old baby is up there."

As they resume public life, the couple is leaning on former royal nanny Jessie Webb, 71, a jovial touchstone from William's own childhood—more proof that they are choosing family over formality. "The last few weeks for me have been a very different emotional experience," said William. "Catherine and now little George are my priorities."

BY GEORGE!

Prince Charles predicted that the new prince will be known as "Georgie in no time." **ABOVE**: Crew members of the British warship *HMS Lancaster* celebrate the news. **BELOW**: William and Kate present George to the world. "I'll remind him of his tardiness when he's a bit older," William jokingly told the waiting mob of photographers, "because I know how long you've all been standing out here."

Leaving 7-week-old Prince George safely at home with his nanny, the duo stepped out to a Tusk Trust awards gala on Sept. 12. The charity's CEO, Charlie Mayhew, said they seemed to be free of new-parent nerves: "I don't think they looked at their mobile [phones] all night!"

SMILE AND SAY 'WENSLEYDALE CHEESE'

Baby George (that's him at the center, in a copy of the lace and satin christening gown originally made for Queen Victoria's daughter in 1841 and worn by more than 60 royal infants) got through his big day with aplomb. Somewhat to his parents' surprise, he stayed mellow through the christening ceremony and the formal photo sessions that followed (seated, from left: Queen Elizabeth II; Prince George; Catherine, the Duchess of Cambridge; Prince William. Standing, from left: Prince Philip; Prince Charles; Camilla, Duchess of Cornwall; Prince Harry; Pippa Middleton; James Middleton; Carole Middleton; Michael Middleton). "Everyone was in a very jolly mood," said a royal source. George "was a happy little bundle of joy."

On April 19, after a four-day manhunt and a police shoot-out, alleged bomber Tamerlan Tsarnaev, 26, was dead and his brother Dzhokhar, 20, was captured hiding in Watertown. On July 10, the once-promising student smirked in federal court as he pleaded not guilty to the 30 charges against him, including using a weapon of mass destruction. He faces the death penalty.

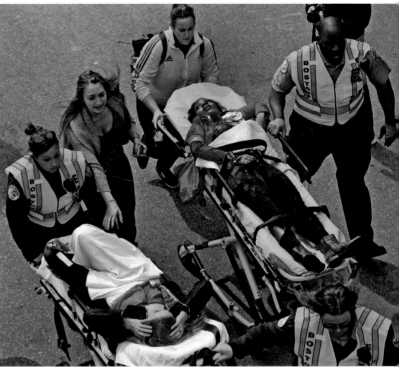

· · · · · ·
· · · · ·

MARATHON BOMBING

Four hours into the 117th Boston Marathon on April 15, as some of the 27,000 runners crossed the finish line to roars from the crowd and hugs from supporters, a boom shook the ground. Ten seconds later, 100 yards away, came a second blast. Screams and acrid smoke filled the air as first responders, runners and strangers rushed to attend to the wounded. Among the crowd were families from Newtown, Conn., there to honor those lost at the school shooting in that town just four months earlier, now witnesses to yet more senseless tragedy.

Despite the confusion and terror, strangers came together to help any way they could: Blood banks were stocked within hours, and Bostonians handed over coats and shirts off their backs. "There were unbelievable injuries," recalled Brian Walker, 49, of Boston. "A woman had glass in her leg. I gave her my coat because she was going into shock, and another guy made a tourniquet out of his shirt to try to stop the bleeding.… Furniture from a café was blown into the street; people who lost limbs were bleeding all over the sidewalk. It looked like a war zone. The smell was horrific … horrible, burning, very ugly, acrid. Smoke everywhere." Runners and spectators searched for loved ones. Steve Cooper, 50, of North Andover, Mass., finished the race and was separated from wife JoAnn during the chaos: "My wife was at the finish line, right there, when the blast hit. I couldn't reach her, so for the next hours, I was running around trying to find her. It was like 9/11: You couldn't make a phone call. She's not answering her phone, and I'm hearing about the dead and injured. I wandered near where we had parked and literally bumped into her. I've never hugged her and cried more."

In the end the attack left more than 144 injured and three dead. Krystle Campbell, 29, from Arlington, Mass., was "a class-A person," said her grandmother Lillian Campbell, 79, of Somerville, Mass. She worked up to 80 hours a week in the food service industry, but still found time to call her grandmother every day. Added Lillian the day after the tragedy: "I missed her calling me today." Boston University student Lingzi Lu, 23, was eulogized by her father as a "jolly girl," who'd dreamed of studying in America. "We hope everyone who knew Lingzi … will help carry on her spirit." Also killed was Martin Richard, 8. The third grader "had this grin, like he always had something funny he was thinking about," said Christina Keefe, a friend in the Richards' tight Dorchester neighborhood, where the family is active in both the kids' school and St. Ann's parish. Martin was on Boylston Street with his mom, Denise, and little sister Jane, who were both hospitalized with serious injuries. Neighbor Jane Sherman saw Denise and the kids that morning as they headed off, and then Martin's father, Bill, when he returned home late that night, driven by a friend. "He was wearing a hospital johnny and was white as a sheet, walking slowly," said Sherman. "I asked, 'Bill, is everything okay?' and he didn't answer. The friend said no, it was Martin that died." The next day Bill composed a statement that read, in part: "Pray for my family."

All told, 16 people lost limbs in the blasts. Minutes before Jeff Bauman, 27, a Costco employee who had come to the marathon to cheer on his girlfriend, lost both of his legs, he had noticed a man in a black cap place a backpack near the finish line. After two days he regained consciousness and "asked for a paper and pen," his brother Chris said, and wrote: "bag, saw the guy, looked right at me." The tip helped the FBI track down Tamerlan Tsarnaev (see box). Celeste Corcoran, 47, lost both of her legs; her daughter Sydney, 18, was injured when shrapnel severed the femoral artery in her right thigh. They recovered in a shared hospital room,

and on May 28 Sydney was crowned prom queen. "She looked gorgeous," said Celeste, a hairdresser. "Every milestone like that, it's like, life goes on. There are times when I'm sad and angry that this had to happen and at the people who did it, but I don't waste my time on them. I dwell on the fact that … my daughter is alive and as hard as it is, I'm still alive—I'm still me. And we're stronger people."

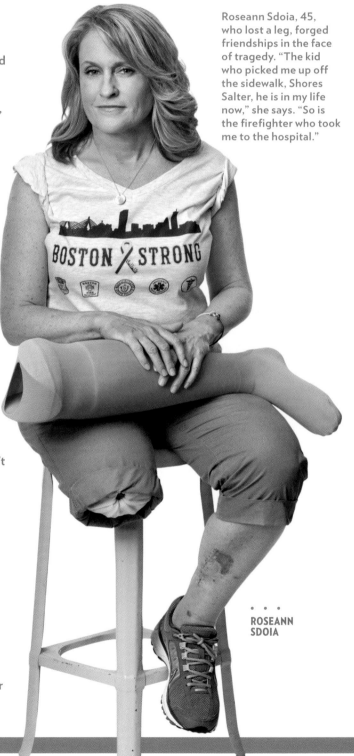

Roseann Sdoia, 45, who lost a leg, forged friendships in the face of tragedy. "The kid who picked me up off the sidewalk, Shores Salter, he is in my life now," she says. "So is the firefighter who took me to the hospital."

• • •
ROSEANN
SDOIA

HEATHER
ABBOTT

MERY
DANIEL

ADRIANNE
HASLET-DAVIS

"I choose to focus on the positive," says Mery Daniel, 31 (left), whose left leg had to be amputated. "I'm happy to be alive." On May 30, the medical school grad and mom was photographed alongside other survivors at Spaulding Rehabilitation Hospital in Charlestown, Mass. Says Daniel: "All of this taught me to really focus on what's important in life." That inspiring outlook is shared by Human Resources Manager Heather Abbott, 39 (right), who lost a foot, and dance instructor Adrianne Haslet-Davis, 33 (center), who lost part of her leg. She went on to be featured on *Dancing with the Stars* and has documented her recovery for CNN. "I insist on being called a survivor, not a victim," she said. "A victim ... means I somehow belong to somebody or I'm suffering because of him. I'm not suffering. I'm thriving."

A BRAVE CHOICE

The jet-set Jolie-Pitts may be the year's highest-earning acting couple, but as the actress and director revealed in a candid *New York Times* op-ed on May 14, their life has not been all champagne and chateaux. On Feb. 16 the mom of six, 38, underwent a preventive double mastectomy after learning she carried a mutated BRCA1 gene predisposing her to cancer. After losing her own mother, Marcheline Bertrand, to ovarian cancer at age 56, Jolie said the operation reduced her chances of developing breast cancer from 87 percent "to under 5 percent. I can tell my children that they don't need to fear they will lose me to breast cancer." Her partner of eight years, Brad Pitt, 50, remained by her side "for every minute" of three operations to remove and reconstruct her breasts in as many months, she wrote, and he called her choice "absolutely heroic." Just five weeks post-surgery, still keeping it private, Jolie traveled to a remote refugee camp in Congo to speak with rape survivors. She plans to have her ovaries removed—to reduce her high risk of ovarian cancer—at a later date. "Life comes with many challenges," she wrote in the *Times*. "The ones that should not scare us are the ones we can take on and take control of." In November she'll receive an honorary Oscar, the Jean Hersholt Humanitarian Award.

SIMON COWELL, BABY DADDY?

The X Factor judge, better known for his yachts, Ferraris and pithy put-downs, may soon be sporting a Snugli. On July 31 came word that Cowell, 54—who in the past has stated his complete disinterest in parenthood—is expecting his first child with Lauren Silverman, 36, the ex-wife of Cowell's former close friend, real estate mogul Andrew Silverman. "I didn't think it was going to happen," admitted Cowell, "But you have to deal with it as a man. Let it happen naturally."

His path to fatherhood has run anything but smooth. Silverman was still married when news of her pregnancy broke and, to add suds to the scandal, Cowell was named a corespondent in Andrew's divorce filing. Under the glare of a tabloid frenzy, the exes, who have a 7-year-old son, finalized their divorce Aug. 14.

Time seems to have mellowed Cowell. In September he told PEOPLE, "I am the happiest now that I have been for a long time." His media empire remains a priority, but Cowell says he's thrilled to have something other than credits attached to his name: "If I dropped dead and the only thing I had were my shows, it would be quite pathetic," he said. "It sounds corny, but you have to have a legacy in life."

A GRIP TOO STRONG

He shot to fame as quarterback Finn Hudson on *Glee*. But on July 13, four years after the hit series premiered, Monteith, 31, was dead at the Fairmont Pacific Rim Hotel in Vancouver, the result of a mixture of heroin and alcohol. Costar Dot-Marie Jones reacted on Twitter: "My heart is broken." The Canadian actor's girlfriend and TV love interest Lea Michele, 27, echoed that heartbreak at the Teen Choice Awards Aug. 11, when she told the audience: "Cory . . . became a part of all of our hearts, and that's where he'll stay forever." For *Glee*'s Oct. 10 tribute episode, she sang—through tears—a haunting rendition of "Make You Feel My Love." Said series creator Ryan Murphy: "Lea was very instrumental in trying to save his life and get him the help that he needed."

Michele was "terrified" when she caught Monteith doing drugs this past spring, said a show source. When he entered rehab in March, she told PEOPLE, "I love and support Cory and will stand by him through this." Said a close friend: "Lea knew he did heroin in his past" but wanted to believe hard drug use was behind him. He may be remembered as a cautionary tale. "If I can . . . shed light on . . . a difficult situation that I know that many kids are experiencing like I did when I was a teenager," said Monteith in 2011, "that's huge." But for his family and fans, his legacy will be what Michele called "his beautiful, beautiful heart."

"He was very special to me and also to the world," said Michele after Monteith's death. Now, says a source close to her: "Just getting up in the morning means remembering Cory is gone." Added costar Jane Lynch: "I know it's just been brutal for her. I never lost a boyfriend when I was 26 years old."

DEEN DEBACLE

It wasn't Paula Deen's first helping of drama. The Queen of Comfort Food's Double Chocolate Ooey Gooey Butter Cake Ice Cream and infamous Lady's Brunch Burger—ground beef patty, fried egg and bacon sandwiched between two glazed donuts—have long raised hackles, and cholesterol, throughout the land. In 2012 the Food Network star copped to a type 2 diabetes diagnosis three years (and countless butter-drenched desserts) after the fact—and at the same time announced she was endorsing a line of diabetes drugs.

The latest flambé ignited after a lawsuit brought by a former employee for sexual discrimination and racial harassment. In a deposition leaked to the media in June, Deen, 66, admitted to using the N-word multiple times in the past. The fallout was swift and brutal—and was not helped by several clumsy video apologies and a tearful mea culpa on the *Today* show. Deen's lucrative business deals fell like dominoes, starting with her 11-year relationship with the Food Network.

Ardent fans were outraged and a "We Support Paula Deen" Facebook page has attracted more than 600,000 likes. Ticket sales for the annual Paula Deen cruise are so brisk that an extra cruise has been added for 2014. Her sons, Jamie, 46, and Bobby, 43, also chefs, whose own cooking shows remain on the air, are her biggest supporters. Said Bobby: "That is not her heart. It is certainly not the home that we were raised in."

A federal judge dismissed the racial discrimination case in August, and a settlement was reached on the remaining claims in the lawsuit. In her first public appearance in three months, Deen received a thunderous ovation at the Metropolitan Cooking & Entertaining show in Houston. Overcome with emotion, she told the crowd, "These are tears of joy, y'all," then joined her sons to cook up a peanut butter pie.

Deen (with Jamie, above left, and Bobby on *The Chew* in Jan.'12), who says "the stove is my safe place," appeared at other Texas cooking demos and celebrated her son's cookbook, *Jamie Deen's Good Food* at a party in Savannah. "My mother has faced every challenge you can imagine," said Jamie. "She refuses to be beaten down."

30 ROCK SIGNS OFF

"I am so glad to be here hosting *Saturday Night Live*," said Tina Fey, 43, during her opening monologue for the show's season 39 premiere on Sept. 28, "because [as] some of you might know, I don't have a show anymore. And unless I'm on TV once every three weeks, a little part of me dies." The 4.8 million viewers who said goodbye to *30 Rock* after seven seasons on Jan. 31 know exactly how she feels. On Sept. 22, Fey won her eighth Emmy, this time for writing *30 Rock*—based on her nine years at *SNL,* where she rose to become its first female head writer—and in the frazzled fashion of her TV alter ego Liz Lemon, inadvertently flashed a nipple from the stage. But unlike Lemon, Fey turned the by-then viral wardrobe malfunction into a punch line, not only on *SNL* but on *Late Night with Jimmy Fallon*, where she "recapped" the moment by showing a photo of a nursing dog. Fey's singular brand of comedy "is like a multiple warhead," said costar Alec Baldwin. "The joke keeps detonating."

So what's next for the blockbuster author (*Bossypants*), movie star (*Date Night*) and woman who, as noted by *Time Style & Design*, "created and nurtured a TV show that was so influential and critically acclaimed, it's amazing it wasn't canceled" and "had a key part in contributing the following words and phrases to the lexicon: Blerg, What the what?! and I want to go to there. Oh, and [gave] birth to two children. Plus, with one dead-on impression, possibly helped decide the 2008 presidential election." For starters, Fey will spend more time with those kids, Alice, 8, and Penelope, 2. "I'll drag them all over," she said of downtime with her daughters. "They're gonna be like, 'Mommy, go back to work!'" She'll do that too: Her next movie is March's *Muppets Most Wanted*. She's adapting her film *Mean Girls* as a Broadway musical. And she'll produce two upcoming TV shows—one about a women's college, the other a workplace comedy. So somewhere inside a TV studio, *30 Rock*-style shenanigans *will* be taking place. If only fans could watch.

HOT DOG $2.00
SAUSAGE $3.00
PRETZEL $2.00
CHEESE PRETZEL $3.00
PIZZA PRETZEL $3.00
JALAPENO PRETZEL $3.00
APPLE CINNAMON $3.00
Spring Water 24oz. $2.00 | Bottled Drinks 20oz.
Gatorade 20 oz. $3.00 | Tropicana Drinks 20oz.
Canned Drinks 12oz. $1.00 | Chips

Tina Fey, with mustard and surrounded by her cast (from left, Tracy Morgan, Alec Baldwin, Jane Krakowski and Jack McBrayer), summed up her show's appeal: "When I first started thinking about *30 Rock, Sex and the City* was just ending," she told IN STYLE. "I really liked it. But I knew I couldn't wear those clothes and I didn't want to shoot sex scenes, so I thought, 'Let's explore the opposite of that.'"

A BOY AND HIS PANTS

"It's basically a joke," Bieber's rep said of the gas mask he sported to "hide his face from the paparazzi."

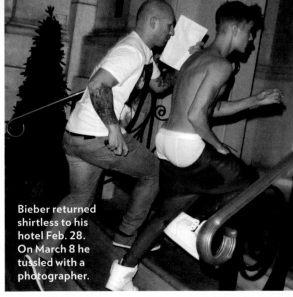

Bieber returned shirtless to his hotel Feb. 28. On March 8 he tussled with a photographer.

From gas masks to exposed drawers, Justin Bieber's outlandish behavior tested the tolerance of even the most faithful Beliebers. In March he lunged at a photographer while leaving a London hospital where he'd been treated for shortness of breath after collapsing onstage. In July a video showed the singer, 19, relieving himself in a restaurant mop bucket, then mysteriously dissing Bill Clinton (Bieber apologized to the former President and tweeted some of his words, with the #greatguy). Just two months earlier Bieber had scolded a booing crowd at the Billboard Music Awards: "I'm an artist and I should be taken seriously, and all this other bull should not be spoken of."

Bieber (with rapper Lil Twist in June) is "wildin' out," said a source who has spent time with him. "On a scale of hot sauce, he's a mild, but his money is so hot, it can get him anything."

His penchant for drop-crotch pants aside, said his rep, "he's not having a breakdown."

MEET BABY KIMYE

Although they were used to an entirely different type of late-night bottle service, Kim Kardashian, 33, and Kanye West, 36, say they've adjusted to their new roles as mom and dad to baby daughter North "Nori" West, born three weeks early on June 15. In fact, the instant she clicked into mommy mode, the reality TV and social media superstar went uncharacteristically quiet. Nesting at mom Kris Jenner's Hidden Hills, Calif., house while her and West's $11 million Bel Air mansion was being renovated, she would not return to a red carpet until Paris Fashion Week in late September. "I'm just loving life a little bit too much at home right now," she explained at the time. West, who spent much of Kim's pregnancy abroad recording his album *Yeezus*, became a hands-on dad overnight, changing diapers, swaddling and singing to Nori. "He hardly ever leaves his girls," says a friend. "He's been documenting everything. He doesn't want to miss a moment." A 10-week-old Nori made her debut in true Kardashian style: West flashed her photo on grandma Kris's talk show Aug. 23. On Oct. 21, West staged an elaborate surprise proposal to his "dream girl" in the middle of San Francisco's AT&T Park. "She's the love of my life," he said that day. "She gave me a beautiful daughter."

SECRET SHARER

As a teen who appeared to live largely by himself in an Ellicott City, Md., condo, Edward Snowden used to sit transfixed in front of his computer. "I could see him through his window working at all hours," said Joyce Kinsey, a former neighbor who describes him as "a well-mannered, nice boy." She was stunned to learn Snowden, 30, is the computer analyst behind two leaks that sent the U.S. intelligence community into a tailspin.

Snowden, who has worked for the National Security Agency and the CIA, released classified documents detailing two NSA surveillance programs authorized by Congress: One gathers the phone records of hundreds of millions of Americans; another monitors the Internet traffic of nine high-tech companies. "I can't in good conscience allow the U.S. government to destroy privacy, Internet freedom and basic liberties," Snowden told Britain's *Guardian* newspaper in outing himself as the leaker. As the Justice Department launched a criminal investigation, Snowden has been granted asylum by Russia and is living in a secret location. If he returned to the U.S., Snowden could face life in prison. "I do not expect to see home again," he said.

TWERK TEMPEST

Of her penchant for pantslessness (above, right) and scandalous VMAs performance, Cyrus told Matt Lauer on the *Today* show Oct. 7: "I mean, it's kind of what I want. I'm an artist, so I'm hoping I get a little attention. [The VMAs] went exactly as planned. I mean . . . we're still talking about it."

ENTERTAINMENT WEEKLY hailed her in-your-face sexy album *Bangerz*, released Oct. 8, as "utterly fresh" and "proof that Miley won't settle for just shocking us." But shock people she did: From the cropped platinum do she unveiled last summer to her tongue-wagging twerk at the MTV VMAs on Aug. 25 (which caused the inventor of the foam finger to rail that she'd "degraded" an "honorable icon"), the former Disney darling, 21, is heck-bent on proving, as she put it, "I can just have fun and not think about any kind of repercussion."

Except for one: Her 15-month engagement to *Hunger Games* hunk Liam Hemsworth, 23, apparently could not withstand her edgy transformation. "Liam thinks that Miley has changed for the worse, and he can't accept it," said a Cyrus insider. Post-VMAs, "he didn't understand why she had to be so provocative." Though Cyrus stood her ground ("I'm going to change. I'm going to be different. I'm going to do what I want to do"), they confirmed their split on Sept. 16. Just a day later Hemsworth was photographed kissing Mexican actress Eiza González. That may have been on Cyrus's mind when she performed her hit "Wrecking Ball" through tears at the iHeartRadio music festival on Sept. 21. "She can't believe he moved on so fast and so publicly," said a Cyrus insider. "But her family and friends keep reassuring her that she made the right decision." After all, it had been a long time coming: Breakup rumors first dogged the pair in February; in May she offered some insight as to why: "I've put too much into this record to put anything else in front of it."

ZIMMERMAN WALKS

On July 13 a jury declared George Zimmerman, the man accused of killing 17-year-old Trayvon Martin, not guilty of second-degree murder. It was a stunning conclusion to a dramatic case that became a referendum on race and gun laws after Zimmerman, a neighborhood watch volunteer, shot Martin, an unarmed black teen, as he walked through a gated Florida community on Feb. 26, 2012. The acquittal resulted in demonstrations across the nation and moved President Obama to comment that "Trayvon Martin could've been me 35 years ago."

Since the acquittal, Zimmerman's wife of nearly seven years, Shellie—who stood by him during the trial—filed for divorce after a domestic dispute on Sept. 9, during which, she claimed, her husband threatened her with a gun. Police found no weapon, and the charges were dropped, but Shellie said on the *Today* show that she didn't know "what he's capable of." Her lawyer said divorce papers have not yet been served because Zimmerman's whereabouts were unknown.

Zimmerman made 46 phone calls to police since August 2004 to report disturbances and attended a citizen's police academy in Seminole County.

..... DEADLY TWISTER

As students at Plaza Towers Elementary School in Moore, Okla. (population: 56,000), were preparing for the end of the school year on May 20, they were interrupted by an announcement over the intercom: "Take cover." Minutes later a deadly EF5 tornado ripped the roof off the school, knocked down walls and sent cinder block and metal flying. Ripping across the Oklahoma City suburb with 200-mph winds, the twister tossed cars and trucks like toys and splintered dozens of homes. By the time it was over, 24 people were dead, 9 of them children. Rescuers rushed to the school, pulling dazed students from the rubble and down a human chain to a triage center in the parking lot, where frantic parents waited. Robert W. Letton Jr., pediatric trauma medical director at the Children's Hospital at Oklahoma University Medical Center, saw about 50 patients under the age of 16: "Part of me was relieved we weren't seeing a huge amount of seriously injured kids, but the other half said that's because we were too late; they were already too far gone." Neighbors worked through the night in hopes of finding victims alive. "We've been through this before," said Tiffany Thronesberry, whose mother's house collapsed. "Everyone just went around helping each other out."

Kelcy Trowbridge (with her brother-in-law Dustin Weher and her three children) looks out on the wreckage. The tornado—later determined to have been the widest twister on record in the U.S.—wasn't the first to hit Moore. So why stay? "We're used to this, just like Californians are used to earthquakes," said elementary schoolteacher Pam Lewis, wife of mayor Glenn Lewis. "We will rebuild. Our whole life is here."

"This isn't going to break up their marriage," says a friend of the couple. Reese (below, in her mugshot) admitted that she was "deeply embarrassed about the things I said."

REESE REGRETS

While lunching with pals in L.A. a while back, Reese Witherspoon—known in Hollywood as a churchgoing mom of three—criticized celeb bad girls who land in hot water behind the wheel. "She was saying, 'How do they keep getting in so much trouble? Get a driver!' " said an eyewitness.

But Witherspoon's straight-arrow reputation veered off course on April 19, when she and her husband of two years, Hollywood talent agent Jim Toth, 42, were arrested in Atlanta following a night out. On a police video that quickly went viral, Witherspoon was seen protesting her husband's arrest, saying, "Do you know my name?...You're about to find out who I am." Witherspoon immediately issued a public apology; privately, friends say, she was humiliated and worried about the fallout. But less than three days later she was back at work, flashing her dazzling smile at the premiere of her new indie film *Mud*. Toth pleaded guilty to a DUI, was fined $600 and ordered to perform 40 hours of community service; Witherspoon pleaded no contest to a charge of physical obstruction and paid a $100 fine.

BEYOND BRAVE

By the time she was 11, Malala Yousafzai was taking on the Taliban by passionately championing Pakistani girls' right to an education. A top-ranked student, Malala gained international recognition after she was revealed to be the anonymous 2009 blogger who exposed the Taliban's reign of terror in the BBC's "Diary of a Pakistani Schoolgirl." "For a young girl to speak up against them," says BBC editor Aamer Ahmed Khan, "is remarkable."

Sadly, the Taliban's response was typically brutal. On her way home from school, two gunmen stopped the bus Malala, then 15, and about a dozen classmates were riding in and shots rang out, injuring three schoolgirls. A bullet pierced Malala's skull and lodged near her spinal cord. After being stabilized, she was flown to Birmingham, England, where doctors replaced part of her skull with a titanium plate. Five months and several surgeries later, she was back at high school in Birmingham.

On July 12th—her 16th birthday—Malala spoke publicly for the first time since her attack, addressing the UN in a call for universal education. "One child, one teacher, one pen and one book," she said, "can change the world."

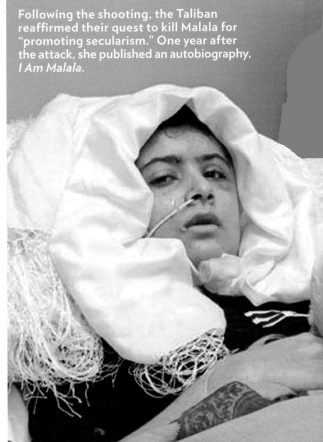

Following the shooting, the Taliban reaffirmed their quest to kill Malala for "promoting secularism." One year after the attack, she published an autobiography, *I Am Malala*.

Malala, who speaks near-perfect English, told a gathering of youth leaders at the UN, "The terrorists thought that they would change our aims and stop our ambitions. But nothing changed in my life except this: Weakness, fear and hopelessness died. Strength, power and courage was born."

Michelle Knight

A CRIME BEY

"I'm Amanda Berry," the frantic young woman told the 911 operator. "I've been kidnapped and I've been missing for 10 years."

With those words, the nightmare in which Amanda; Gina DeJesus, kidnapped in 2004; and Michelle Knight, taken in 2002, had been trapped began to lift. Almost unbelievably, all had been held prisoner in a ramshackle Cleveland home, its garage covered in barbed wire and windows reinforced with Plexiglas, by Ariel Castro, a bass player in a local Latin band. Also held captive was a 6-year-old girl, born to Berry and fathered by her abductor. Evidence recovered from the house attests to their enslavement: 99 ft. of chains, padlocks weighing a total of 92 lbs. After one escape attempt, one of the women was chained to a basement pole with an electrical

MISSING

IF YOU HAVE ANY INFORMATION ABOUT AMANDA:
CALL THE CLEVELAND, OHIO FBI (216) 522-1400
OR THE POLLY KLAAS® FOUNDATION (800) 587-4357

AGE PROGRESSION TO 26 YRS. BY NCMEC

Amanda Berry
Missing from Cleveland, OH

Date Missing: 4/21/03
Date of Birth: 4/22/86
Age at Disappearance: 17 years
Race: Caucasian
Sex: Female
Height: 5'1"
Weight: 110 lbs.
Eyes: Brown
Hair: Sandy Blonde, long.
Other: Surgical scar on lower abdomen and pierced left eyebrow.
Last Seen Wearing: Burgundy Burger King shirt, black pants and a black hooded jacket.

Amanda was last seen walking home from work at the Burger King at W. 110th and Lorain in Cleveland, Ohio on April 21, 2003. She has not been seen or heard from since

AMANDA IS BELIEVED TO BE ENDANGERED.

A Service of the Polly Klaas Search Center - Flyer Revised March 2013 www.pollyklaas.org

Si Ud tiene alguna información, por favor llame a la Policía de Cleveland, FBI (216) 522-1400

WELCOME HOME GIN

Gina DeJesus

Amanda Berry

OND BELIEF

cord around her neck. On July 4, 2012, Castro let them sit on the porch to watch fireworks with wigs on their heads—and a gun pointed at their backs.

Berry finally escaped after neighbor Charles Ramsey heard her screaming for help, dashed up the steps and kicked out a door panel. In the weeks that followed, details emerged of the unthinkable horrors the women had endured, including physical and sexual abuse, temperature extremes and games of Russian roulette. At Castro's August sentencing hearing, the 4'7" Knight told the man who had chained her, beat her and induced miscarriages after raping her: "Now your hell is just beginning. I am not going to let you define me."

Rescuer Charles Ramsey

"I'm not a violent person," Ariel Castro, 53, the former school bus driver who for more than a decade tortured Michelle Knight, 32, Amanda Berry, 27, and Gina DeJesus, 23, told a Cleveland court on Aug. 1, when he was sentenced to life without parole plus 1,000 years. "I just kept them there against their will." On Sept. 3 he was found hanged in his central Ohio prison cell.

Ariel Castro

Using photos (like the one above) from former classmate Diane O'Meara's Facebook page, Tuiasosopo created a profile for the fictious "Lennay Kekua" that fooled Te'o (right).

THE LADY VANISHES

Manti Te'o, a star linebacker for Notre Dame, was convinced he'd met the love of his life: Lennay Kekua was religious, beautiful and a family-oriented person with Polynesian roots like himself. They'd been Facebook friends since 2010, but when they tried to meet, according to Te'o, Kekua would make various excuses. Then in April 2012, she was in a car crash that left her in a coma. Te'o called the hospital often; his girlfriend's siblings told him his voice quickened Kekua's breathing. She miraculously woke up, then was diagnosed with leukemia. On Sept. 12, within 24 hours of Te'o's grandmother's death, Kekua died. Only after his tragic story went public did Te'o learn something else about his love: She never existed.

Te'o got "catfished," an alarming trend in online fraud. How could a star athlete with a 3.2 GPA be duped? "She referenced names of relatives and family members . . . in such detail," Te'o's parents told People, "that there was no reason to doubt her."

A California man, Ronaiah Tuiasosopo, confessed that he created Kekua; later, on the *Dr. Phil* show, he said he had fallen in love with Te'o. Meanwhile, Te'o has definitely moved on: In May he began his NFL career by signing a four-year, multimillion dollar contract with the San Diego Chargers.

A CRY FOR HELP

In March, Paris Jackson seemed a smiling cheerleader at the private Buckley School in Sherman Oaks, Calif. But by June, Michael Jackson's daughter, 15, was confined to L.A.'s Children's Hospital after attempting suicide by cutting her wrist with a knife and swallowing 20 ibuprofen.

It was a shocking turn in the life of a teenager who broke hearts when she called Michael "the best father you can imagine" in a tearful speech at his 2009 memorial service. Despite her attempts to forge a normal life, sources say the teen has been battling depression for a while. Her home life has hardly been stable—her family has fought over her guardianship—and Paris has been targeted by cyberbullies, who, according to a source, say "horrible things, like 'Michael is not your father, so go kill yourself and die.'" Hovering over it all is Paris's witnessing her father's fatal heart attack when she was just 11. "She was probably hit the hardest," said her brother Prince. "She was my dad's princess."

Paris continues to be "a danger to herself," a source told PEOPLE. After leaving the hospital she was transferred to an undisclosed residential treatment center.

GOODBYE, SCI

Leah Remini, the star of *The King of Queens* for nine seasons, had been a Scientologist since she was 9 and was one of the church's most vocal members. Then, at fellow Scientologist Tom Cruise's 2006 wedding to Katie Holmes, she asked a seemingly simple question: Where was Shelly Miscavige, wife of the church's leader, David?

According to sources, Remini was promptly warned not to ask about Miscavige, who hasn't been seen in public since 2007. Church officials call the anecdote "ludicrous," but there were reports that Remini had been required to undergo an "attitude-modification process."

On July 11 news broke that Remini had split from the church. Later she told PEOPLE that "no one is going to tell me how I need to think; no one is going to tell me who I can, and cannot, talk to."

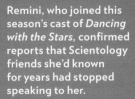

Remini, who joined this season's cast of *Dancing with the Stars*, confirmed reports that Scientology friends she'd known for years had stopped speaking to her.

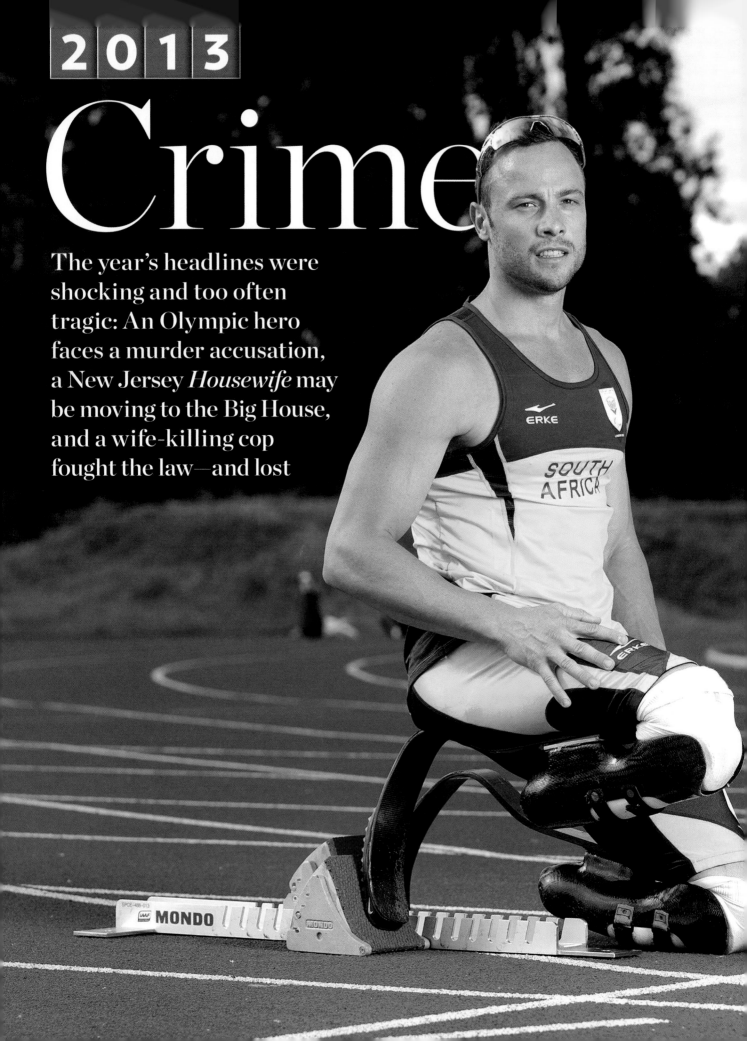

2013 Crime

The year's headlines were shocking and too often tragic: An Olympic hero faces a murder accusation, a New Jersey *Housewife* may be moving to the Big House, and a wife-killing cop fought the law—and lost

OLYMPIAN ON TRIAL

He's known as the Blade Runner, the double-amputee sprinter who thrilled crowds with his explosive performances on J-shaped prostheses at the 2012 London Olympics. She was a 29-year-old law school grad, a top model and aspiring reality TV star who was also an activist for women's empowerment. A-listers in South Africa, Oscar Pistorius and Reeva Steenkamp, who had been dating for four months, turned heads wherever they went. But if a man's gaze lingered on his girlfriend too long, Pistorius would grow jealous, according to Steenkamp pal Maddie Sims. Often during their courtship, Sims witnessed Pistorius, 26, growing agitated if free-spirited Steenkamp was late to meet him; if she wore her hair in a ponytail or was dressed too casually; if she asked a waiter too many questions. "Many things that made Oscar a great athlete made him difficult to live with," she said. "He was very focused, very intense, very assertive." But, she added, "he was loving 95 percent of the time, so that's what we thought the majority of their relationship was."

Now Pistorius is facing 25-years-to-life after shooting Steenkamp in the head, hip, arm and hand through a locked bathroom door in his Pretoria home. Pistorius maintains he mistook Steenkamp for an intruder and shot in self-defense; prosecutors say they have witnesses who will testify that they heard a woman's screams before the sound of gunshots. Released on bail within a week, Pistorius was formally indicted in August. The trial is set for March 3.

Whatever the truth, the runner's image is in tatters, shredded by police and press accounts that Pistorius has a trigger temper, a love of guns and a history of incidents at his house—including "allegations of a domestic nature." In fact, there were reports that security guards investigated a disturbance at his address earlier that night. And Steenkamp's promising career, which had her poised to become a leading TV personality, "will never materialize," said her uncle Mike Steenkamp. "Everything that she was doing has come to an abrupt end. It's tragic."

On the morning of her death, Steenkamp (with Pistorius on Feb. 7) was to have addressed a high school audience. "Accept who you are," part of her notes for the speech read. "Be brave."

"He started a legacy," U.S. Paralympic sprinter Blake Leeper said of Pistorius (below, walking to a police car after the shooting, which made headlines around the world). "I'm not sure he'll be able to finish it the way he wanted to."

REAL HOUSEWIFE, BIG TROUBLE

Their table-flipping tempers and gaudy lifestyle made them reality stars, but on July 29, after 39 felony fraud and tax-evasion charges were filed against *Real Housewives of New Jersey* star Teresa Giudice, 41, and her husband, Joe, 43, they faced the prospect of moving from a Towaco, N.J., mansion to prison. In a 33-page indictment, prosecutors chronicled the illegal lengths to which they say the Giudices scrambled in order to keep up the lavish life they led on-camera. Each fraud charge carries a maximum penalty of 30 years in prison and a $1 million fine. "The Giudices lied," said U.S. Attorney Paul Fishman. "That's reality." Their trial is set for February.

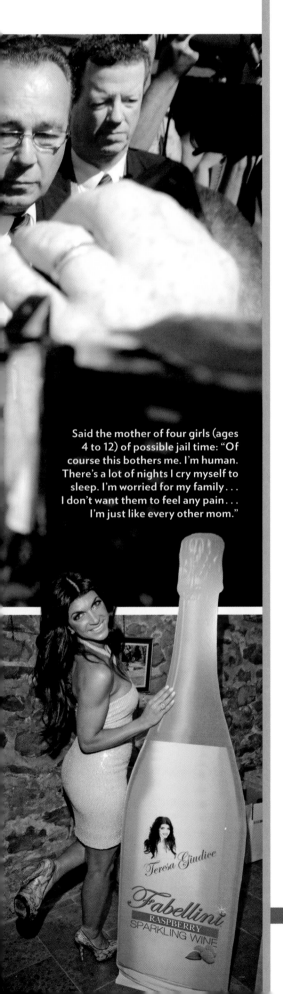

KILLED BY HER BEST FRIENDS

Bubbly and smart, with a great sense of humor, Skylar Neese had a wide circle of friends at her Morgantown, W.Va., high school, but only two she considered her BFFs. So when the 16-year-old suddenly went missing in July 2012, it was only natural that the pair would help her parents, Dave and Mary Neese, scour the area and post Facebook messages begging her to come home.

Both girls knew that she never would. In January, six months after Skylar vanished, one of those supposed best friends, Rachel Shoaf, 17, stunned the small community of 30,000 by confessing to police that she and another girl had lured Skylar out one night, driven 30 miles to a remote area in Pennsylvania and stabbed her to death. Unable to bury the body, they dragged her to the side of the road and covered her in branches. In exchange for leading authorities to Skylar's remains and offering the most incomprehensible of motives—they just didn't want to be friends with her anymore—Shouf was charged as an adult and given a reduced charge of second-degree murder. Prosecutors have recommended a 20-year sentence, but she could get up to 40 years behind bars.

Shouf's alleged accomplice, Sheila Eddy, has never confessed and pleaded not guilty to first-degree murder. Now 18 and also being tried as an adult, she remains in custody awaiting trial, scheduled to begin in February. "She's still saying she didn't do it, while she was the mastermind," said Dave Neese, who with Mary visits a bench and memorial built where Skylar's body was found. "It has been like hell times a million."

After Skylar Neese (below) vanished, friends began to suspect Sheila Eddy (above). In science class, recalled one, Eddy and Rachel Shoaf would say under their breath "how much they hated Skyler."

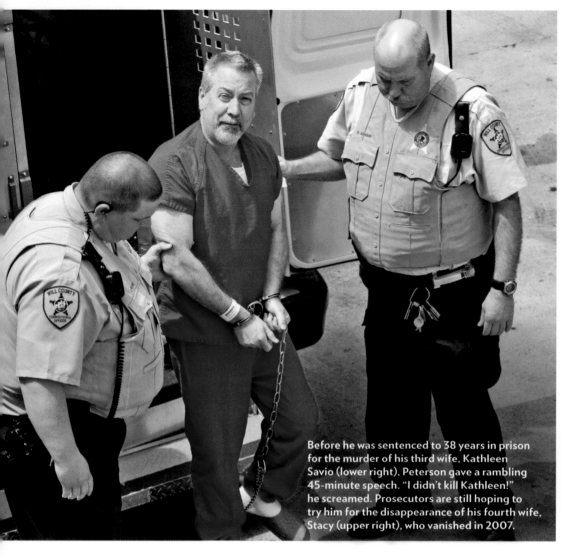

Before he was sentenced to 38 years in prison for the murder of his third wife, Kathleen Savio (lower right), Peterson gave a rambling 45-minute speech. "I didn't kill Kathleen!" he screamed. Prosecutors are still hoping to try him for the disappearance of his fourth wife, Stacy (upper right), who vanished in 2007.

DREW PETERSON STOPS LAUGHING

The former cop appeared confident he would never be convicted. When his estranged wife, Kathleen Savio, 40, was found dead in a bathtub in her Bolingbrook, Ill., home in '04, Peterson claimed she drowned. When his fourth wife, Stacy, went missing in '07—and a second autopsy showed Savio had struggled—he denied any involvement. When, two years later, he was finally arrested for Savio's murder, he quipped, "I should have returned those library books." And that wasn't the end of his shtick. The next day he was led into his arraignment in a red jail jumpsuit and manacles. "Three squares a day and this spiffy outfit," he cracked. "How can I complain?" Peterson, 59, remained so self-assured at his murder trial that in August, when the judge considered granting a mistrial after prosecutorial missteps, he requested that the trial continue.

When a jury found him guilty of murder on Sept. 6, Peterson showed no emotion. Not so Savio's family. "You can finally rest in peace," her half brother Nicholas Savio, 31, said he later whispered at her grave. "Your coward killer has been brought to justice."

"They're worth millions," says Rotterdam public prosecutor Barbara van Unnik of the pieces believed burned by Olga Dogaru—who, along with her son, faces a 20-year sentence. "But that is only a fraction of their cultural, historical value."

Paul Gaugin's *Girl in Front of Open Window* (1898, above) and Pablo Picasso's *Harlequin Head* (1971) were among the artworks stolen in one of the most spectacular art heists in decades.

PICASSO & MONET, UP IN SMOKE?

Some mothers will do anything to protect their children—including, allegedly, incinerating $24 million of artwork stolen from Holland's Kunsthal museum in Rotterdam. Prosecutors believe that when Olga Dogaru found out that her son Radu and five others were charged with stealing seven paintings in October 2012—including works by Mattisse, Picasso, Monet and other masters—she burned them in her home oven in Carcaliu, a Romanian village of 3,400. "The idea became trapped in my mind that if the pictures could not be found, there will be no evidence," she told police. "I sense I made a big mistake."

Or, as art-security expert Anthony Amore put it, "a horrifying crime against culture." Torching such treasures is so unthinkable that officials initially didn't believe Dogaru, who, indeed, reversed herself in a July 22 court appearance, insisting, "I did not burn them." But after forensic testing of the ashes by Romania's National History Museum, its director Ernest Oberlander-Tarnoveanu told PEOPLE, "The evidence is clear." Experts found traces of mineral pigments and blacksmith-forged nails consistent with those that would have been used by Monet or Gauguin. "It's beyond my imagination why someone would do this," he said. As one source close to the investigation ventured, "Mothers from Romania love their sons very much." (Radu and two others later pleaded guilty.)

FOR HER IT'S ALWAYS SHARK WEEK

Conservationist Ocean Ramsey (yes, her real name) vividly remembers her first time swimming unprotected with sharks. "To touch them was breathtaking, one of the most beautiful moments of my life," says the Hawaii-based scuba instructor, 27, who now travels the world swimming with the creatures, hoping to dispel the notion that they live up to their *Jaws* reputation. "Sharks are not mindless man-eating machines," says Ramsey, who had the chance to prove her theory with a 17-ft. great white who let her "tail ride" off Baja, Mexico. Her YouTube video of the encounter—"A Blonde and a Great White Shark"—has been viewed more than 2 million times and will, Ramsey hopes, raise awareness of the shark's plight: 100 million of them are killed yearly. Though sharks are "quite shy" and she has never had a single bite or near miss, Ramsey does caution that more landlubberly types should not try this at home: "For an average person to just jump in wouldn't be wise."

2013
Gallery

Sharks, celebrities, squirrels, a beach boy
Boss and Queen Elizabeth II's space heater:
photos that made us look twice

BEACH BOSS
. . .

What is happening to our rock stars? Where's the decay? The physical manifestation of a million miles and nights on the road? Bruce Springsteen, damp and smiling on a Rio de Janeiro beach, seemed to show a shocking disrespect for cherished stereotypes. And it only got worse: Three days later, on his 64th (!) birthday, the Boss hit the stage at the Rock in Rio festival and delivered a blistering three-hour set that included all the cuts on his 1984 album *Born in the U.S.A.* When he finished, at 3 a.m., delirious fans were asking themselves, "Is this any way for a Social Security–eligible rocker to act? And look?"

OUT OF HER SHELL

· · · ·

When MTV needed a slammo opening act for their Video Music Awards, the go-to gal was, no surprise, Lady Gaga, who, clad in a clammy bikini, gave a rousing, if shellfish, performance.

TEA FOR TWO?

• • •

You're the Queen of England. You can decorate any way you want. And you choose: tan plaid carpet, slipcovered chairs, a dog bed, a stuffed corgi and a space heater in front of the fireplace? Just so, as became clear in this unusually candid picture of Queen Elizabeth II in her sitting room at Balmoral. Her guest, New Zealand Prime Minister John Key, who'd been invited with his family for a weekend visit, was apparently unaware that, per protocol, he was expected to keep mum about his time with Her Majesty—and never, *ever* release any pictures. Nonetheless, royal watchers— who scoured the photo for details (that's Queen Victoria to the left of the mantel and her beloved Prince Albert to the right; Prince William, the Duchess of Cambridge and baby Prince George got a prime spot on a side table behind Key) were mesmerized.

TALK TO THE ANIMALS

Something squirrelly was going on in Manhattan's Washington Square Park, where Katie Holmes struck up a conversation with a loquacious local: All in a day's work filming *Mania Days*, in which Holmes plays a manic-depressive poet.

SOMEONE TO WATCH OVER ME
• • •

Nashville's 5'2" Hayden Panettiere, 24, and 6'6" Ukrainian heavyweight boxer Vladimir Klitchko, 37, may see things eyeball-to-sternum—at least from her perspective—but that didn't stop them from having a fine romance. In October, Panettiere confirmed that they were engaged.

AL PACINO

• • •

Yea, and the funk did settle upon him, albeit briefly: Actor Al Pacino, previously known mostly for his range and intensity, flashed some smoothish moves at a concert by the band Chicago at L.A.'s Greek Theater. Why? To film a scene for his upcoming movie *Imagine*, in which he plays an aging rock star.

KATE PLUS 8

• • •

Made famous—then infamous—by their reality show *John & Kate Plus 8,* the Gosselin sextuplets and their older twin sisters were spectators, with the rest of the world, to their parents' ugly split. Chaos and deprivation seemed to be in the cards when the show was cancelled in 2011. Well, guess what? The sextuplets, now 9, and the twins, 13, are doing just fine. In small-town Pennsylvania, they are doing their homework and their chores, saying grace and getting braces with no brattiness allowed. Kate has primary custody and cobbles together income from her cookbook and website. Finances are tight, she admitted to PEOPLE in August, but the family is tighter. "There is no strife in this house," said the busy mom, on "civil" terms with her ex. "We've gone on happier than before." Says Cara, the quieter twin: "We're all adjusted, and it's normal now."

The Gosselin crew: (front row, left to right)Leah, Alexis, Joel, Aaden, mom Kate. (Back row) Mady, Collin, Hannah, Cara.

2013 Weddings

At intimate gatherings in picturesque French towns and lavish affairs with star serenades and blooms galore, celebs from Keira Knightley to Michael Jordan said 'I do'

Kristin Cavallari
. . .
Jay Cutler

One broken engagement and an adorable baby later, former *The Hills* star Kristin Cavallari and Chicago Bears quarterback Jay Cutler finally made it official on June 8 at a Nashville wedding the bride described as simple, warm and cozy. "It was absolutely perfect," she told PEOPLE. So was 10-month-old son Camden Jack, who was pulled down the aisle in a wagon by a flower girl. "Everyone thought it was just the cutest thing," gushed Cavallari. "I can't wait to see pictures!"

After the vows, 140 guests celebrated with a family-style southern menu including chicken biscuits and grits. As the crowd continued dancing to a Motown band, the newlyweds snuck off to their honeymoon suite. "We were just like, 'We can't believe we did it!'" Cavallari says, laughing. Their brief split "made us realize how much we meant to each other," she says. "We weren't ready to get married two years ago. But now everything is right."

Keira Knightley
· · ·
James Righton

Hundreds of guests? Twelve-foot train? So not Keira Knightley's style. Instead the British actress pulled off her big day in a far smaller way, with a May 4 ceremony at the Mazan town hall in Provence, France. The star, 28, and her rocker fiancé of a year, Klaxons keyboardist James Righton, 29, said "Oui"—and "I do"—in a 30-minute French and English ceremony presided over by mayor Aime Navello. In a Chanel haute couture dress, Karl Lagerfeld jacket and Chanel flats, "Keira looked beautiful," said an observer. A few dozen guests, including Sienna Miller, celebrated at Knightley's vineyard in Mazan. Now comes life as Monsieur and Madame. "My parents are together after 40 years," the actress told *Marie Claire*. "I think it gets more interesting, or I hope so."

Diana DeGarmo
· · ·
Ace Young

"I'm over the moon with happiness," said Diana DeGarmo about her June 1 wedding to fellow *American Idol* finalist Ace Young. Said the equally lovey-dovey groom: "Today was the best day of my life. Diana and I are in it forever." Season 5 heartthrob Young, 32, and season 3's runner-up DeGarmo, 25, had the wedding of their dreams in front of 250 guests at the Luxe Sunset Boulevard hotel in Los Angeles. From the guitar-shaped groom's cake to the yellow and purple motif, "they wanted to put their personal touch on the wedding," said planner Renée Strauss. "We all worked together to make sure every detail was special."

That included DeGarmo's form-fitting Sareh Nouri gown with pearls and rhinestones and Young's custom-made box suit with a crest designed by Strauss: the couple's monogram with "Forever Young" emblazoned underneath. For the first dance, the couple wrote an original song, "I Do." "This is just the start," says Young. "We'll spend our lifetime creating things together."

Jimmy Kimmel
· · ·
Molly McNearney

The guest list at the July 13 nuptials of Jimmy Kimmel and Molly McNearney in Ojai, Calif., read like a talk show host's dream lineup: Ben Affleck, Jennifer Aniston, Emily Blunt and, of course, Matt Damon, Kimmel's viral-video buddy. But just before the wedding kicked off, the groom was pranked by *Precious* actress Gabourey Sidibe, who walked down the aisle in a white dress and veil, pretending to be the bride. Who orchestrated the joke? The real bride, a co-head writer of *Jimmy Kimmel Live*.

Kate Winslet
• • •
Ned Rocknroll

Their romance began with high drama when a fire broke out at Richard Branson's Caribbean house, where Kate Winslet, her then-boyfriend Louis Dowler and Ned Rocknroll were staying in August 2011. Winslet carried Branson's 90-year-old mother to safety and all the guests escaped unscathed. And when it came time to return to New York, it was Rocknroll, not Dowler, who accompanied her, according to Britain's *Daily Mail*.

Rocknroll—who is Branson's nephew and works for his uncle's Virgin Galactic company, which sells space travel packages—was then spotted with Winslet in New York and Paris. According to reports, the pair moved into a 15th-century house in a hamlet in West Sussex, England, in September.

The Oscar-winner, 37, and Rocknroll, 34, tied the knot in secret in December 2012. They exchanged wedding bands by Charles Goode in front of Winslet's two children, Mia, 12, and Joe, 9, and close friends and family. According to British media reports, Leonardo DiCaprio gave away the bride in a ceremony so secret that the bride and groom's parents didn't know about it. Winslet previously was married to Sam Mendes and Jim Threapleton. Rocknroll had been wed to heiress Eliza Pearson, the daughter of Viscount Cowdray. As for his peculiar name? According to his ex-wife, it was all done as a bit of fun. Kate Rocknroll, anyone?

Michelle Kwan
. . .
Clay Pell

Nailing a triple lutz in front of millions without batting an eye? Check. Walking down the aisle without shedding tears? Not so fast. "I thought I would at least make it to the vows, " a laughing Michelle Kwan, 32, told PEOPLE the day after her wedding to national-security strategist Clay Pell, 31. "It was a dream."

The Olympic champ wore a Vera Wang gown; Pell, a Coast Guard Lieutenant, wore full dress uniform for the Jan. 19 ceremony, held in Providence, R.I. After sharing their self-written vows before 240 family and friends—including Olympic champions Brian Boitano, Dick Button and Dorothy Hamill—the pair spontaneously kissed before the officially scheduled moment. "A few minutes later," a guest said, "the minister said, 'And for their second first kiss as Mr. and Mrs. Clay Pell,' and everyone laughed."

After walking under an arch of sabers formed by Pell's Coast Guard friends, the couple led guests in lighting sparklers before dinner and dancing began. Boitano, 49, spoke at the reception. "It was hard because I couldn't look at her too much because I get kind of emotional," Boitano told PEOPLE. "It's like a little sister growing up. She is truly filled with so much grace on and off the ice."

"I never was one who believed in love at first sight," Kwan told PEOPLE in September. "But I have to admit it happened. I felt there was a magnetic connection between us. I thought he was the one from the beginning."

Melissa Gilbert
· · ·
Timothy Busfield

"Passion, fire, love: Red says all of those things to me," said Melissa Gilbert, 49, who took her third trip down the aisle with *thirtysomething*'s Timothy Busfield in a stunning scarlet gown featuring a fitted bodice and a softly draped, tiered skirt. Gilbert, the *Dancing with the Stars* alum, searched high and low for a dress before spotting it at Morgane Le Fay in Santa Monica. "The moment I saw it, I knew," she said.

Gilbert and Busfield, 55, who has also been married twice before, had known each other for 20 years before getting engaged over the Christmas holidays. On April 24 they wed at San Ysidro Ranch in Santa Barbara. "Tim and I are fairly unconventional, so I felt white was uncalled for," said the red-haired Gilbert. "When I walked out, the expression on Tim's face told me I had made the right choice!"

Halle Berry
· · ·
Olivier Martinez

Six years ago the twice-divorced Halle Berry told InStyle, "I will never, never get married again." Then she met French actor Olivier Martinez. On July 13 he became husband No. 3 when the two wed in Vallery, France. Sixty guests—including Berry's 5-year-old daughter Nahla, who wore a floral wreath in her curls—watched the couple exchange vows in a civil-service union followed by a religious ceremony at the village chapel. Then festivities commenced at the luxe Château des Condé, where dinner in the arbor was capped off by a fireworks display. But the real showstopper occurred on Oct. 4 in L.A., when the pair welcomed their son Maceo-Robert

Kelly Clarkson

• • •

Brandon Blackstock

Their original idea was an "earthy" backyard affair for 200 guests, but Grammy-winner Kelly Clarkson, 31, and music manager Brandon Blackstock, 36, "got so overwhelmed" by all the decisions that they decided to elope. On Oct. 20 they pulled off their secret ceremony on a bucolic Tennessee farm with just a minister and Brandon's two kids (with ex-wife Melissa) in attendance. "Our whole life is a celebration," the former *American Idol* winner said. "We don't need another day where we throw a big party. We would rather have an intimate moment that's special."

Michael Jordan
· · ·
Yvette Prieto

NBA legend Michael Jordan wanted to give his bride "everything she's ever wanted," said an insider. The result? Thousands of flowers, a crystal-studded cake and serenades from Usher and K*Jon. Three hundred guests—including Tiger Woods, former Chicago Bulls teammate Scottie Pippen and onetime rival Patrick Ewing—watched Jordan, 50, and Yvette Prieto, 35, walk down the aisle of Bethesda-by-the-Sea church in Palm Beach, Fla., on April 27. "There was a feeling of incredible love between them," said one observer.

The reception, coordinated by wedding planner Sharon Sacks, was held in a tent nearly the size of a football field that was bedecked with white roses, peonies and tulips. Crystal candelabras and candles added to the romance. The bride, a former model, chose a J'Aton Couture gown adorned with Swarovski crystals. Crystal broaches also glittered from the seven-layer white rum cake. And because the bride "adores" Robin Thicke, says a source, Jordan surprised her by having him sing too.

With all the extravagant touches, it was the newlyweds who left the lasting impression, said a source: "They are so very much in love."

Sean Parker
• • •
Alexandra Lenas

Tech titan Parker, 33, who made
billions from Facebook and
Napster, wed singer-songwriter
Lenas, 24, in an over-the-top,
$9 million wedding held among
the redwoods in Big Sur, Calif.
Complete with fake waterfalls,
faux stone walls and a bridge,
the event "was pure magic,"
said Parker's rep.

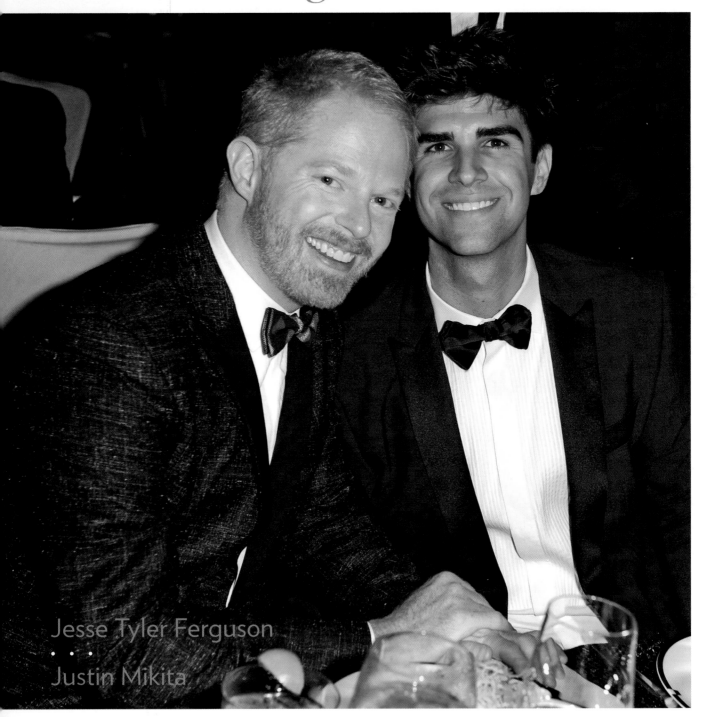

Jesse Tyler Ferguson
• • •
Justin Mikita

The *Modern Family* star, 37, who plays uptight lawyer Mitchell Pritchett on the Emmy-winning show, wed real-life attorney Justin Mikita, 27, in New York on July 20. Playwright and screenwriter Tony Kushner officiated as famous friends—including *Family* costar Julie Bowen and Nigel Lythgoe, Cat Deeley and Mary Murphy from Ferguson's *So You Think You Can Dance* guest-judging gig—looked on. "I think the service at Justin and Jesse's wedding was so beautifully honest," Lythgoe later tweeted. "It was so emotional that when we weren't laughing we were crying." Bowen later dubbed it the "#bestweddingever." Not to be outdone in the tweetfest, the happy couple chimed in early Sunday morning. Justin summed up his happiness with just a single word: "Husband." And Jesse's tweet? "Never been happier. XO Goodnight!"

Bethany Hamilton
. . .
Adam Dirks

Bethany Hamilton had a few jitters on the morning of her Aug. 18 wedding, so the 23-year-old survivor of a famous 2003 shark attack did what comes naturally: "I went surfing on the beach where I first surfed with one arm," she said. Hours later, she took a moment to "just sit in my car before going down the aisle. So many emotions were rushing through me." Hamilton, wearing a Lazaro gown, exchanged vows with youth-ministry volunteer Adam Dirks, 25, on a Kauai estate surrounded by plumeria, orchids and 300 guests. After the ceremony, the newlyweds shared their first dance to Ben Harper's "The Three of Us." "I love surfing," said Hamilton, "but it doesn't compare to getting married."

Tina Turner
• • •
Erwin Bach

Let's get the obvious over quickly: Love had a *lot* to do with it. After 27 years together, Tina Turner, 73, and her partner, German music producer Erwin Bach, 57, decided to tie the knot at their home on Switzerland's Lake Zurich. Female guests, including Oprah Winfrey, were asked to wear white; gents like Bryan Adams, who sang the couple down the aisle, to go black-tie. Turner, who became a Swiss citizen in April, went with Armani. "I've reached my nirvana," she said, "that happiness that people talk about when you wish for nothing."

Avril Lavigne

. . .

Chad Kroeger

For her July 1 wedding to Nickelback frontman Kroeger, singer Averil Lavigne, 28, had a simple plan: "Make sure it's a crazy vacation," she told *Hello* magazine, "and an experience of a lifetime for our guests."

So, after finding a medieval castle near Cannes and a black tulle Monique Lhuillier gown, the Canadian lovebirds had a goth-themed ceremony before 110 guests and a three-day party. Rock on.

2013

Engaged

Glee's Matthew Morrison tweeted it, Whitney Houston's daughter took to Facebook and The Bachelor and Bachelorette shouted it from the small screen: 'We're getting married!'

Sean Lowe

Catherine Giudici

Bucking a long tradition of *Bachelor* breakups, Lowe, 30, a Dallas-based entrepreneur and Giudici, 27, a Seattle graphic designer, are heading full-speed toward matrimony. Since Lowe competed on *Dancing with the Stars*—he was eliminated during week 8—the couple has been spending time away from the spotlight, traveling and hammering out details for their Jan. 26 wedding, which will be televised live. "I've just never been able to open up to anybody the way I have with him," Giudici told PEOPLE. "He's a man, but he's so compassionate. The full package." Says Lowe: "When we're together, we know it's right."

Matthew
Morrison
• • •
Renee Puente

What could be more gleeful? Matthew Morrison's engagement to model Renee Puente, 30, was announced in June by their friends Elton John and David Furnish at their White Tie and Tiara Ball in London. According to Eonline, Coldplay's Chris Martin joined John to serenade the couple, who have been dating since 2011, with a duet of "Your Song." Morrison, 35, later tweeted: "I'm going to marry my best friend! Happy day for me and @Renee_Puente."

Bobbi Kristina Brown
• • •
Nick Gordon

They were raised under the same roof after her parents, Whitney Houston and Bobby Brown, took in Gordon when he was 12, more than a decade ago. But Bobbi Kristina Brown, 20, wants to make one thing perfectly clear: She is not keeping it all in the family. "I'm tired of hearing people say, 'Eww your [sic] engaged to your brother,'" she wrote in a Facebook rant on July 10. "We aren't even real brother and sister, nor is he my adoptive brother." What would her mother, who died in 2012, think of their engagement? "Mommy was the one who even said that she knew that we were going to start dating," she wrote. "My mom knows me better than any of you." No wedding date has yet been set.

Desiree Hartsock
· · ·
Chris Siegfried

"Blindsided" when Brooks Forester spurned her affections in front of 7.8 million viewers, *The Bachelorette*'s Desiree Hartsock didn't wait long for her happy ending. During the next week's episode the bridal stylist, 27, accepted the proposal of Seattle mortgage broker Chris Siegfried, 27. "Brooks's leaving gave me clarity—I had been falling in love with Chris," said Hartsock, who had a message for all those yelling "rebound!": "I didn't settle."

Lauren Conrad
· · ·
William Tell

"You don't want a slob," Lauren Conrad once said. "But you don't want a guy who is constantly borrowing your tweezers."

And that guy is (apparently): William Tell, 33, a law student and musician, and the apple of Conrad's eye for more than a year. "I am very excited to share with you guys that William and I got engaged over the weekend," the former star of *The Hills*, now an author and fashion designer, wrote on her blog on Oct. 13. "I am beyond thrilled."

"Everyone is so happy for her. He's such a great guy. They are perfect for each other!" a source told PEOPLE.

As befits a former reality star, the details of the upcoming nuptials—no date so far—will likely not be hush-hush. Noted Conrad, 27: "Get ready for lots more wedding content [on my blog] as we begin the planning process,"

2013
Couples

Whether just starting out or patching up a decades-long marriage, these couples said 'I Will' to love

Danny DeVito
• • •
Rhea Perlman

The sun shined a little brighter when Danny DeVito and Rhea Perlman, who shocked fans when they announced a split in October 2012, were back together again after five months apart. Long one of Hollywood's most beloved and enduring couples, they began quietly working on their relationship, and in December, DeVito hinted at a reconciliation, telling *Extra*, "We're working [on the marriage]. Rhea and I are really close." The *It's Always Sunny in Philadelphia* star, 69, and the former *Cheers* actress, 65, have been married for 31 years and have a son and two daughters, all in their 20s. "They love each other," said a friend of the couple. "Always have and always will."

Tiger Woods
· · ·
Lindsey Vonn

Forget the mega-yacht, the mega-mansion and his reputation as one of history's greatest golfers. Ever since his sex scandal four years ago, Tiger Woods has not exactly been lucky in love. His squeaky-clean image and his marriage to Elin Nordegren imploded amid allegations of escorts, salacious text messages and no fewer than 12 women claiming to have slept with him. "I have let my family down and I regret those transgressions with all of my heart," he wrote on his website.

But after a 45-day rehab (reportedly for sex addiction), counseling and finalizing a multimillion dollar divorce settlement, Woods, 38, seems to be on the rebound. On March 18 he revealed on Facebook that he is dating skiing champ Lindsey Vonn, 29. In a simultaneous post, the Olympic gold medalist wrote, "Our relationship evolved from friendship into something more . . . and it has made me very happy."

Vonn, who split from her husband of four years, Thomas, in November 2011, seems unfazed by Woods's bad-boy past. "They have sat down and talked it out more than once," said a source close to Woods. "He has explained his side and owned up to what he did wrong."

The couple, who met in April 2012, have spent quality time together since February, when Vonn seriously injured her knee during a World Cup race in Austria. Woods flew her home on his private jet and was at her side during surgery. Between rehab work, Vonn has been spotted aboard Wood's yacht *Privacy* and Jet-Skiing with his kids over Memorial Day. Woods, meanwhile, had an impressive year, winning the 2013 PGA Tour Player of the Year Award.

In August, Vonn returned to the slopes, and is planning to compete in the 2014 Winter Olympics in Sochi, Russia. Will Woods be there? "He's hoping to come," she said. "He's kind of a fish out of water in the cold weather. It's going to be really cute!"

2013
Splits

Kristen Stewart and
Robert Pattinson;
Bruce and Kris Jenner;
and George Clooney
and Stacy Keibler are
some of the celebs who
uncoupled in 2013

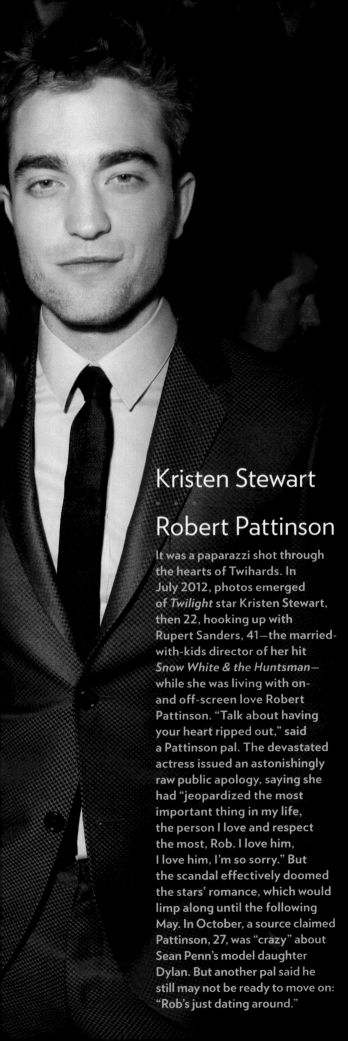

Kristen Stewart

Robert Pattinson

It was a paparazzi shot through the hearts of Twihards. In July 2012, photos emerged of *Twilight* star Kristen Stewart, then 22, hooking up with Rupert Sanders, 41—the married-with-kids director of her hit *Snow White & the Huntsman*—while she was living with on- and off-screen love Robert Pattinson. "Talk about having your heart ripped out," said a Pattinson pal. The devastated actress issued an astonishingly raw public apology, saying she had "jeopardized the most important thing in my life, the person I love and respect the most, Rob. I love him, I love him, I'm so sorry." But the scandal effectively doomed the stars' romance, which would limp along until the following May. In October, a source claimed Pattinson, 27, was "crazy" about Sean Penn's model daughter Dylan. But another pal said he still may not be ready to move on: "Rob's just dating around."

George Clooney

Stacy Keibler

Original Bachelor George Clooney has kissed yet another girlfriend goodbye: The Oscar winner, 52, and former pro wrestler Stacy Keibler, 34, split in July after two years. Why? "Stacy called it quits," said a source close to the couple. "She wants to have children and a family someday. She knows where George stands on that." ("I've always known fatherhood wasn't for me," Clooney said in 2011. "That's why I'll never get married again.") With work commitments keeping them on separate continents, it became clear that the *Gravity* star and the host of Lifetime's *Supermarket Superstar* "have less in common than they thought," said a pal.

Kris Jenner
· · ·
Bruce Jenner

In the six years they've been on television, the Kardashian-Jenner clan has lived for drama—from a sex tape to unplanned pregnancies, a drawn-out divorce and a DUI. But ask Bruce and Kris Jenner what's to blame for their separation following 22 years of marriage, and their answers seem uncharacteristically low-key for a family that has parlayed fevered tabloid headlines into a multimillion-dollar industry. Talking to PEOPLE on Oct. 9, a jovial Kris chirped, "We're just happier living apart. It's a modern-day family!" Her estranged hubby, contentedly ensconced in the Malibu pad he's occupied since June, sounded equally sanguine: "There is no animosity," he said. "Life is good!" Healthiest separation ever or some seriously good acting? Stay tuned.

Josh Brolin
· · ·
Diane Lane

It was a Valentine's Day to remember—for all the wrong reasons. On Feb. 14, Diane Lane, 48, ended her eight-year marriage to Josh Brolin, 45. "This was a hard decision for both of them," said a source. Said Brolin's father, James, at the Oscars Feb 24.: "Everything is mutual. It's all okay." Despite a rocky start— Lane and Brolin made headlines following a domestic dispute four months into their marriage— things were back on track by 2005 when Lane told PEOPLE, "I feel much better having a strong man with me who makes me feel embraced and secure." Sadly, that wasn't enough to make it last. "Sometimes they seemed happy and fine together," said an insider of the couple, who were raising three kids, "but things more often seemed tense between them. They didn't seem to have a balanced relationship."

Bethenny Frankel
· · ·
Jason Hoppy

For the pair, whose whirlwind courtship, surprise pregnancy and shotgun wedding were documented on-camera for Bravo's *The Real Housewives of New York City, Bethenny Getting Married?* and *Bethenny Ever After,* it's a sad but unsurprising end to an often rocky relationship. Frankel, 43, admitted that her intense work life—including her Skinnygirl empire and a new daytime talk show—"may have exacerbated our issues." The divorce has turned nasty—at stake is her fortune (estimated by Forbes at $55 million in mid-2011) and custody of their daughter Bryn, 3. "It's ironic," she said. "By the time you're reading fairy tales to your kids, you're discovering they might not come true."

Dina
Eastwood
• • •
Clint
Eastwood

When they married 17 years ago, he was a Hollywood legend; she was a local news anchor more than three decades his junior. But Clint Eastwood, 83, and wife Dina, 48, made it work—living happily in Carmel, Calif., and raising their daughter Morgan, 16. (Eastwood has six older children and one previous marriage.) But things began to unravel, according to sources, when Dina, Morgan and Francesca Eastwood (Clint's daughter with actress Frances Fisher) filmed a reality show, *Mrs. Eastwood and Company*. (It was cancelled after one season.) Clint made a few appearances, but he was "furious," said a source. "It went against everything he stands for—he's incredibly private, and she put his kids on TV." As word of the breakup spread, Dina defended her estranged husband: "He is a wonderful, good-natured, brilliant person," she tweeted. "No matter what, I attest to that."

Carey Lowell
• • •
Richard Gere

He likes to meditate, she prefers
parties; after 11 years Richard
Gere, 64, and Carey Lowell, 52,
"simply grew apart," said a friend.
The couple has been separated
for some time, according to the
New York Post, with Gere, a devout
Buddhist, preferring the solitude
of their Bedford, N.Y., home,
while Lowell socializes from
their historic mansion in North
Haven, N.Y. Parents to son
Homer, 13, the couple will
"do everything possible
to keep things amicable,"
said a friend, "and put
their child first."

Jane Lynch
· · ·
Lara Embry

She continues to steal scenes on *Glee* as the acerbic tracksuited Sue Sylvester, and in May she made her Broadway debut as Miss Hannigan in *Annie*—but Jane Lynch's real life hit a big bump. On June 10 the actress, 53, and psychologist Dr. Lara Embry, 44, announced the end of their three-year marriage. In July, Lynch said that their breakup is "not dramatic," but then Embry asked for a reported $94,000 in monthly spousal support. One thing remains intact: Lynch's bond with Embry's daughter Haden, 11. Said a source: "Jane loves that little girl, and that relationship will continue."

Orlando Bloom
· · ·
Miranda Kerr

In the middle of his Broadway run in *Romeo and Juliet*, of all things, actor Orlando Bloom and his onetime Juliet, model Miranda Kerr, dropped the curtain on their three-year marriage. In October they announced they had separated but would still "love, support and respect each other" and be loving parents to son Flynn, 2. Many around them had seen it coming, noting that Bloom had moved out of the couple's New York City apartment three months earlier. "They started out great, but they are so different," said a source close to the pair. The low-key Bloom, 36, avoids the spotlight, while Aussie Kerr, 30, ranked by Forbes as the second highest-paid model in the world, travels constantly promoting a beauty line and wants to start acting. "She's very focused on furthering her career." Nonetheless, the day after the announcement the trio was spotted on Fifth Avenue. "Orlando and Miranda looked happy and affectionate with each other," said an observer. "It didn't look like the split was bad."

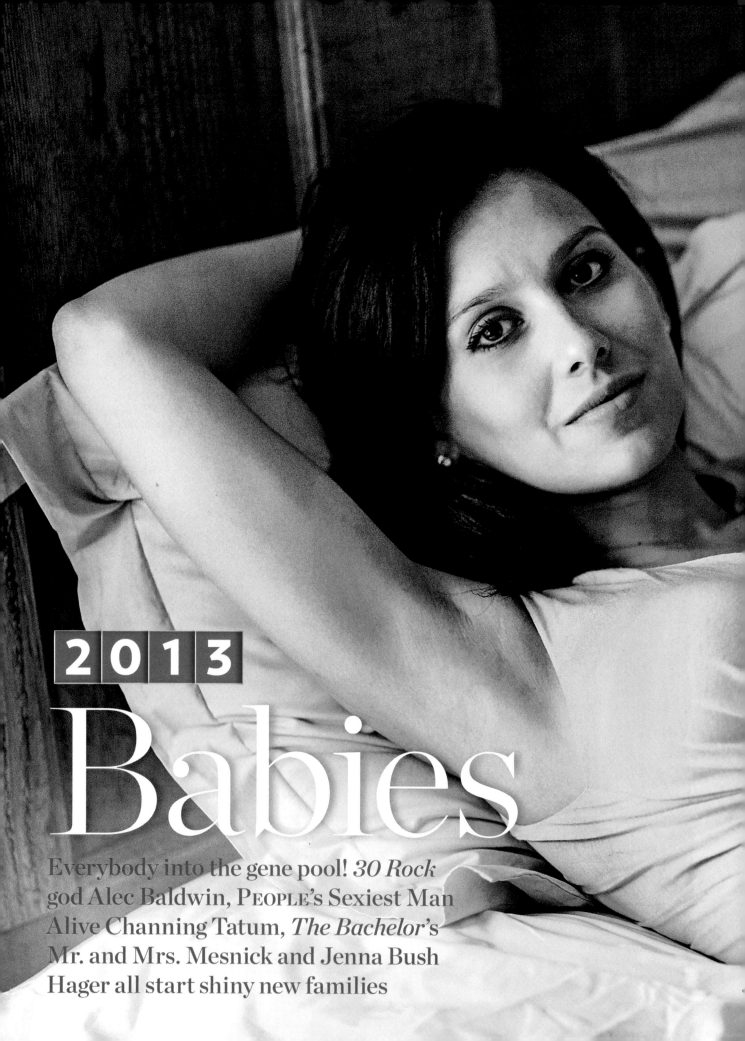

2013 Babies

Everybody into the gene pool! *30 Rock* god Alec Baldwin, PEOPLE's Sexiest Man Alive Channing Tatum, *The Bachelor*'s Mr. and Mrs. Mesnick and Jenna Bush Hager all start shiny new families

Alec Baldwin
· · ·
Hilaria Thomas

Well before the August 23 arrival of Carmen Gabriela Baldwin, her dad, actor Alec, was lobbying for a change in title. "At this point, he thinks he's going to be Mr. Mom," said his skeptical wife, Hilaria, 29. "We'll see at 3 o'clock in the morning, when the baby is screaming and we need to change the diaper, if he's going to be Mr. Mom at that point." Baldwin, 55, a king of TV comedy after seven seasons of *30 Rock*, swore it was so. "My dream is to be home with the baby, standing in the doorway saying goodbye to Mommy," he said. "Mommy is going to work now. Bye, Mommy...don't work too hard!"

Alas, it was not to be. Two weeks later it was announced that Baldwin, for two seasons the host of the WNYC podcast *Here's the Thing*, was getting his own nighttime talk show on MSNBC.

Channing Tatum
. . .
Jenna Dewan-Tatum

Just two months after welcoming daughter Everly on May 31, Jenna Dewan-Tatum, 32, was back at work, filming TV's *Witches of East End.* But she's had some seriously sexy support from husband of four years Channing Tatum, 33. He's "been amazing," the new mom said of the movie star who has played the role of "set husband," taking care of Everly while Dewan-Tatum filmed. "You see the thing you love the most with the other thing you love the most, and there's just a natural new awakening of the love you guys share together," the actress added. (There you have it: Babies—the only thing that can make Tatum, PEOPLE's reigning Sexiest Man Alive, even sexier). "Those first few months, it's just ridiculous, just [taxing]," said Tatum. "All I can really do is just sit there and change diapers . . . and get them food. Whatever they want."

Jason Mesnick
· · ·
Molly Mesnick

Soon after their daughter Riley Anne was born on March 14, People sat down with the reality TV couple at their Kirkland, Wash., home. "I love watching Molly with her," said Jason Mesnick, 36. "That awe of loving someone so much." For the Mesnicks, who married in 2010, the expansion of their family has been a happy new chapter (Riley's big brother is Ty, 8, a son from Jason's first marriage). The couple connected on *The Bachelor* in 2009, but Jason, a businessman, first proposed to Melissa Rycroft before having a change of heart and begging Molly, a marketing executive, for a second chance. "After that we haven't looked back," said Molly, 29, adding that there is one lingering issue: "Jason got me a baby book, and one of the pages is 'This is how Mommy and Daddy met.' That will be an interesting conversation, to say the least."

Jenna Bush Hager
· · ·
Henry Hager

There are good hair days, and there are spectacularly *memorable* hair days. Former First Daughter Jenna Bush Hager figured her fresh blowout would be seen only by the pals at her baby shower. Then her water broke in the middle of it. "It was like a romantic comedy!" recalled the *Today* show correspondent, 31. The bonus—other than the April 13 arrival of 6 lb. 15 oz. Margaret Laura Hager, named for her grandmothers and known as "Mila"—was that Mom looked impossibly put together in the hospital photos.

"I've learned that you can love somebody in a totally different way," she exulted. Investment banker husband Henry, 35, was "a really modern dad" who read Mila her first book, while her own dad, former President George W. Bush, was a tougher sell. "He said, 'Bring that baby back when she can talk.'" Then Dubya made Mila laugh—for the first time. "She laughed at him and that's it. They're in love."

Movies

With the future of the world at stake, the White House under constant attack and the good guys lost in space, everyone—and that includes you, Iron Man—could have used a minion or two

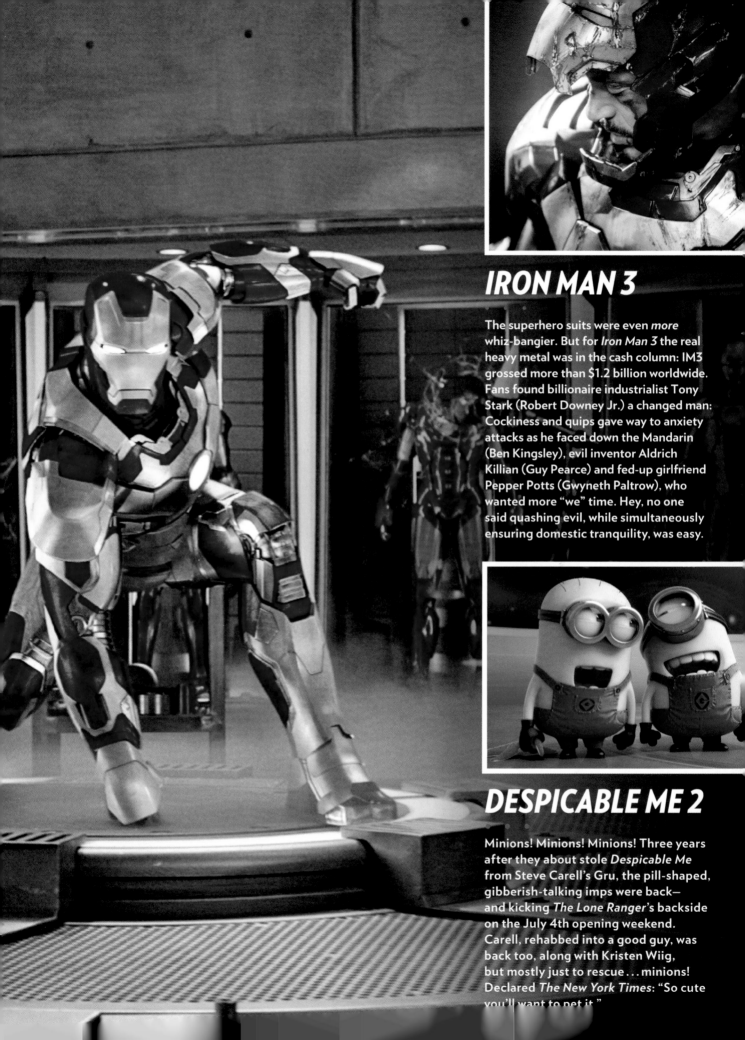

IRON MAN 3

The superhero suits were even *more* whiz-bangier. But for *Iron Man 3* the real heavy metal was in the cash column: IM3 grossed more than $1.2 billion worldwide. Fans found billionaire industrialist Tony Stark (Robert Downey Jr.) a changed man: Cockiness and quips gave way to anxiety attacks as he faced down the Mandarin (Ben Kingsley), evil inventor Aldrich Killian (Guy Pearce) and fed-up girlfriend Pepper Potts (Gwyneth Paltrow), who wanted more "we" time. Hey, no one said quashing evil, while simultaneously ensuring domestic tranquility, was easy.

DESPICABLE ME 2

Minions! Minions! Minions! Three years after they about stole *Despicable Me* from Steve Carell's Gru, the pill-shaped, gibberish-talking imps were back—and kicking *The Lone Ranger*'s backside on the July 4th opening weekend. Carell, rehabbed into a good guy, was back too, along with Kristen Wiig, but mostly just to rescue...minions! Declared *The New York Times*: "So cute you'll want to pet it."

BLUE JASMINE

• • •

What if it all fell apart tomorrow? After Alec Baldwin goes to jail for a Bernie Madoff–like crime, wife Cate Blanchett begins her searingly portrayed spin downward. How low will she go? In his saddest, most scathing film since *Manhattan*, director Woody Allen left it up to us.

GRAVITY

• • •

Two astronauts—Sandra Bullock and George Clooney—are untethered in space. In Alfonso Cuarón's visual stunner Earth looked both familiar and eerily otherworldly. Dodging deadly debris and the fallout of a personal tragedy was a very game Bullock, who made working in zero gravity look like nothing.

MAN OF STEEL

WORLD'S END!

E.T. has left the planet! Intergalactic goodwill gone! Instead, news from the sci-fi zone revealed a dearth of mirth on Earth, under threat of extinction by everyone from zombies—Brad Pitt's *World War Z* (left)—to *Man of Steel's* Kryptonians to *Star Trek into Darkness* and its beloved Klingons, in this prequel still clinging stubbornly to the idea of destroying the human race. Earthlings involved in all three, however, celebrated: *Z* became the biggest grossing movie of Pitt's career; *MOS* proved so popular that Superman is next teaming up with Batman (gasp!); and those Klingons? Another near miss can only mean . . . Hey! Give us another shot!

STAR TREK INTO DARKNESS

WHITE HOUSE WOES

• • •

Compared to the cavalcade of Armageddons (see *World War Z et al.*, above), *Olympus Has Fallen* and *White House Down* might almost qualify as boutique films: They are, after all, only positing the destruction of 1600 Pennsylvania Avenue. So how did the vote go at the box office? Citizens of movieplex made *Olympus*, with Aaron Eckhart as the kidnapped President and Gerard Butler as the disgraced Secret Service agent who saves him, a modest hit. Three months later, however, the competition fizzled; even with certified hunk Channing Tatum on hand to save President Jamie Foxx, fewer moviegoers wanted to take the *White House* tour. As campaign advisers would say: a classic case of message fatigue.

OLYMPUS HAS FALLEN

WHITE HOUSE DOWN

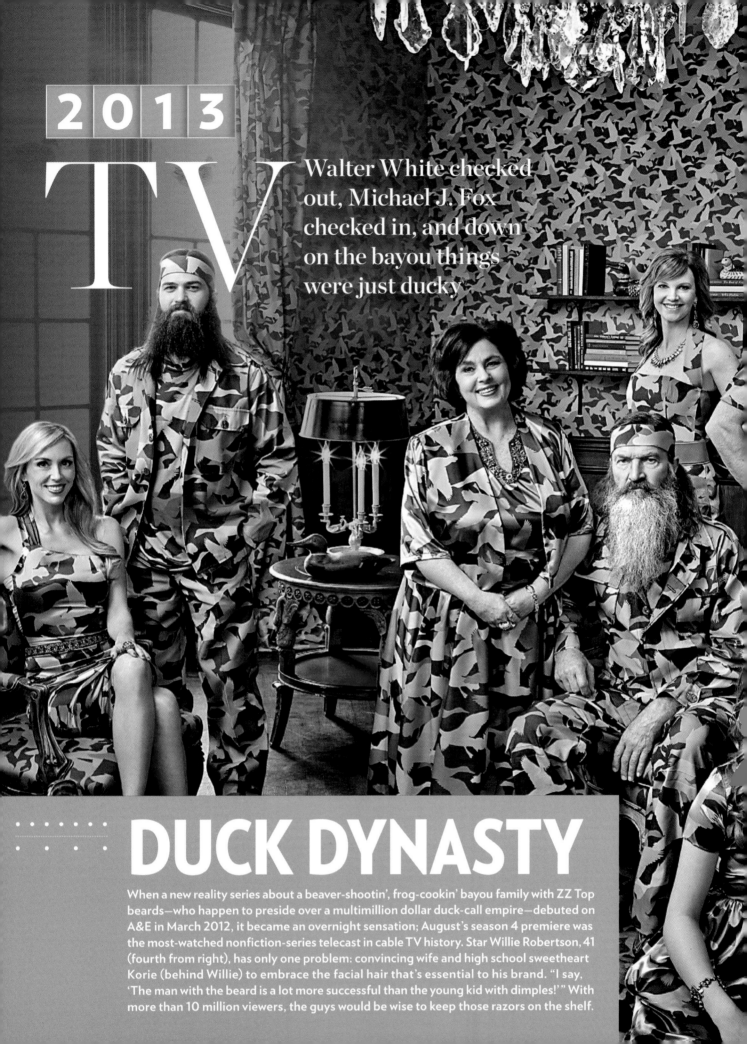

2013 TV

Walter White checked out, Michael J. Fox checked in, and down on the bayou things were just ducky

DUCK DYNASTY

When a new reality series about a beaver-shootin', frog-cookin' bayou family with ZZ Top beards—who happen to preside over a multimillion dollar duck-call empire—debuted on A&E in March 2012, it became an overnight sensation; August's season 4 premiere was the most-watched nonfiction-series telecast in cable TV history. Star Willie Robertson, 41 (fourth from right), has only one problem: convincing wife and high school sweetheart Korie (behind Willie) to embrace the facial hair that's essential to his brand. "I say, 'The man with the beard is a lot more successful than the young kid with dimples!'" With more than 10 million viewers, the guys would be wise to keep those razors on the shelf.

BREAKING BAD

Wanted: The next great TV antihero riding into town on the next classic series. Because AMC's *Breaking Bad*, which followed Walter White (Bryan Cranston) on his strange desert odyssey of drugs, despair and death, came to an end after five seasons. The finale, if perhaps a bit nicer than it should have been, was a major event. Dang, Don Draper, Walt White made you look *puny*.

THE MICHAEL J. FOX SHOW

Some performers don't know when to leave. Others—and this includes Michael J. Fox—we'd prefer would hang around forever. The 52-year-old actor returned to NBC, home of his old sitcom *Family Ties*, in a warm, modest new series about a news anchor dealing (as does Fox) with the challenges of Parkinson's. Fox wasn't asking for pity or indulgence. We just had to show up and let him do his job.

THE MILLION SECOND QUIZ

• • •

Hosted by Ryan Seacrest, this NBC trivia competition was expected to be a reality gorilla as it played out, on and off camera, for nearly 12 days in Manhattan. It was all so preposterously complicated, viewers clocked out before some dude won $2,600,000. A giant slot machine would have been fine.

SCANDAL

• • •

Washington, D.C., never had time to shut down on *Scandal*. The second season of this political melodrama had fans (proudly identified as Gladiators) firing off tweets over the wild plot twists of the latest episode. Kerry Washington, as powerful consultant Olivia Pope, just couldn't seem to decide whether or how to douse the torch she carried for her old boyfriend, the President, who'd been put in the White House by a cabal that included the First Lady. It's the Oval Office in the age of "Oh, no you didn't!" And it's swell.

GAME OF THRONES

• • •

A howl of disbelief rose up across America June 2: The HBO fantasy series killed off—that is: *butchered*—several key characters in the biggest shock of 2013. The episode is now known as "Red Wedding," but you can call it "Thrown by *Throne*."

HOW I MET YOUR MOTHER

• • •

Mom, is that you? For its ninth and last season, the hit CBS sitcom finally revealed that titular woman, destined to marry Ted (Josh Radnor)—that implicit titular man. Played by Cristin Milioti, she arrived bearing homemade cookies. Just like Mom.

ROBIN THICKE

• • •

Every summer's bounty includes The Song, that perfectly potent combination of simple melody, dance-tastic beat, racy lyrics, a racier video that's also pretty hilarious and much-discussed controversy over matters of taste and such. First it is propelled everywhere—absolutely everywhere—into the cosmos, then it wends its way inward, snaking, unstoppable, into your brain. Sleep is pointless; wake up, and like *Groundhog Day*, it's still there. So let's be perfectly clear: Robin Thicke's "Blurred Lines" was The Song, 2013.

2013
Music

Katy Perry scored again, Justin Timberlake and Jay Z took each other on tour, and the line between guilty summertime pleasure and inescapable brain invader was—yes—blurred

KATY PERRY AND LADY GAGA

She's got legs: Perry's *Prism*, her first album since 2010's *Teenage Dream*, entered the Billboard charts at No. 1, one of the best debuts by a woman this year. Her "Roar" also hit No. 1. Lady Gaga's single "Applause" topped out at No. 4; at press time the world was still waiting to see if *Artpop*, the much-anticipated follow-up to her monster 2011 album, *Born This Way*, would confirm that Gaga still had her mojo workin'.

MACKLEMORE AND RYAN LEWIS
• • •

From their album appropriately titled *The Heist*, the Seattle-based rapper and producer Lewis stole the No. 1 spot from Bruno Mars with "Thrift Shop," the first indie song to hit the top slot in nearly 20 years. Both Microsoft and Miller Lite grabbed "Can't Hold Us" (also No. 1) for ads before "Same Love" became a gay-friendly cultural touchstone. Gents: Nap time!

BRUNO MARS
• • •

After the worldwide hits "Just the Way You Are" and "Grenade," Bruno Mars's second outing, *Unorthodox Jukebox* and its No. 1 hits "Locked Out of Heaven" and "Gorilla," proved the Hawaii native king of the new old-school: sharp hooks, boss threads, cool moves, great hair, *SNL* hosting gig. Someone this unafraid of being an entertainer with a capital E can be headed only one place: the Super Bowl.

JUSTIN AND JAY Z

• • •

They had such a good time dueting at the Grammys that blue-eyed soulster Justin Timberlake and rap godfather Jay Z, not content to be the undisputed masters of their separate domains, came together for something even bigger: the ultimate hip-pop road show. The 12-city Legends of the Summer tour found the pair sharing the stage and an 18-piece band, trading off JT classics like "Cry Me a River" and cuts off his album *The 20/20 Experience* with Jay Z hits like "99 Problems" and songs from his *Magna Carta . . . Holy Grail*. Raved *Billboard*: "There was no one-upmanship, just camaraderie, not competition, [just] two guys that work well together . . . as if they had been making music together for years."

Famous for what Jodie Foster called her "rapid-fire teenage-boy-humor brain," Jennifer Lawrence showed some of her signature sass at the Academy Awards nominees' luncheon on February 4. "This year, I'm like 'Suck it up, wear a corset,'" she told the assembled press of her Oscar dress plans. "I am going to go for fashion this time....I never care. Now, I will. Fashion!"

She shoots—she scores! Clad in an ivory-and-blush Dior Haute Couture gown, the It Girl (thanks to the $408 million-grossing *Hunger Games*) glided seamlessly to superstar status when she was named Best Actress for *Silver Linings Playbook*. But her walk to the stage was the stuff anxiety dreams are made of: She tripped. As the crowd rose for a standing ovation, the then 22-year-old joked: "You guys are just standing up 'cause you feel bad that I fell." Same girl. *Great* dress!

2013
Fashion

Stars from Kerry Washington to Blake Lively brought their A-game to the red carpet, and FLOTUS's fringe made headlines, but it was Miley's makeover that got tongues wagging

Great Gowns

Jessica Alba
• • • •

At the Golden Globes the star channeled old Hollywood glamour in sherbet Oscar de la Renta and Harry Winston jewels—but added a modern touch with this Roger Vivier clutch.

Kerry Washington
• • •

In romantic Marchesa at the Emmys, PEOPLE's "Best Dressed Woman in the World" was sheer perfection.

Charlize Theron
• • •

The actress wowed at the Oscars in simple and sophisticated Dior Haute Couture, complemented by platinum Harry Winston jewels and her new chic crop.

Dramatic trains, opulent details and sheer panels helped these six fashion plates make jaw-dropping turns on the red carpet

Rihanna

The singer went surprisingly demure but was still striking at the Grammys in a flowing Azzedine Alaïa chiffon gown and ombre waves.

Jennifer Lopez

The words "understated" and "bombshell" rarely belong together, but they meshed perfectly for Lopez in an embellished, nude Zuhair Murad at the Golden Globes.

Blake Lively

With a plain bodice and dramatic feathers, this Gucci Premiere gown (with Lorraine Schwartz jewels) proved a perfect blend of elegance and edge at the Met Ball.

DIANA STARKOVA

● ● ●

She is, per her website, a "Ukrainian supermodel, beauty queen and auto racing driver." She is also, apparently, a flamenco dancer.

FLORENCE WELCH

● ● ●

Dot's incredible! Whether you call it fashion or a faux pas, no question she got herself spotted.

HANA MAE LEE

● ● ●

Actress Hana may be trying to out Gaga Gaga. Plus: There's a Beavis and Butt-head joke in here somewhere.

ON SECOND
Thought...

To all those who believe it is far, far better to have tried and failed than simply to have worn black, we salute you!

ADELE
· · ·
It only *looks* like the fabric on your grandma's favorite chair; it's actually high-style from Valentino Haute Couture.

ZOSIA MAMET
· · ·
Perhaps a tad *too* minimalist for most occasions, but just right for that medical exam.

KATIE PRICE
· · ·
The heck with neigh-sayers: The U.K. reality star—and girl of Mr. Ed's dreams—was promoting her line of equestrian clothing.

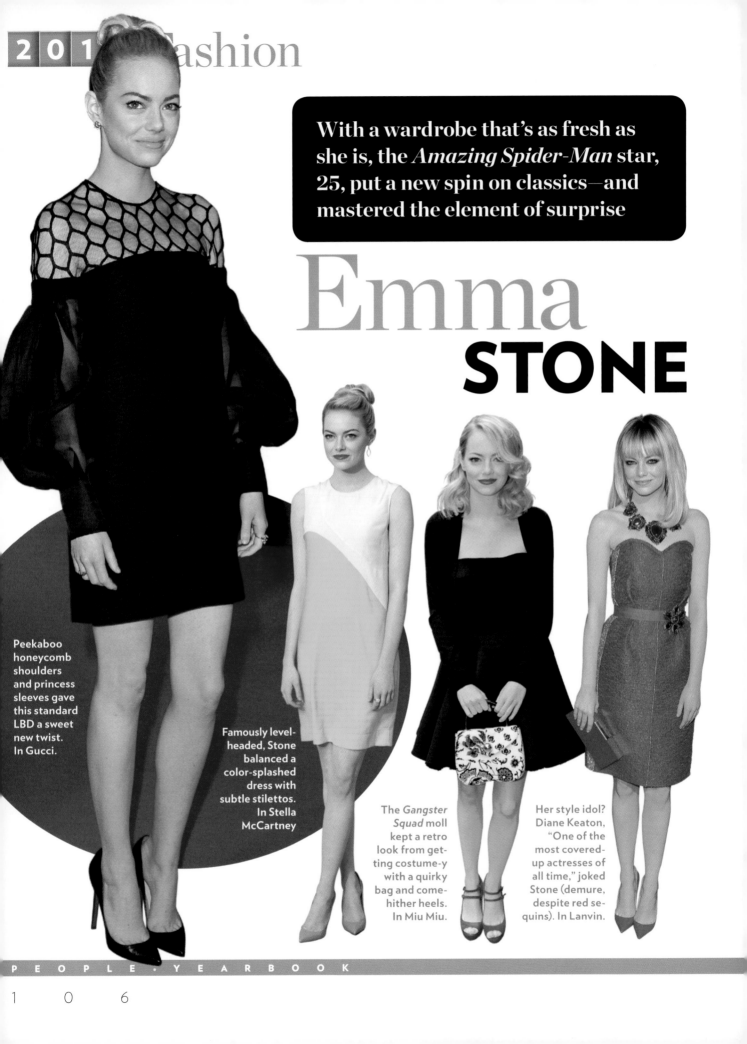

With a wardrobe that's as fresh as she is, the *Amazing Spider-Man* star, 25, put a new spin on classics—and mastered the element of surprise

Emma STONE

Peekaboo honeycomb shoulders and princess sleeves gave this standard LBD a sweet new twist. In Gucci.

Famously level-headed, Stone balanced a color-splashed dress with subtle stilettos. In Stella McCartney

The *Gangster Squad* moll kept a retro look from getting costume-y with a quirky bag and come-hither heels. In Miu Miu.

Her style idol? Diane Keaton, "One of the most covered-up actresses of all time," joked Stone (demure, despite red sequins). In Lanvin.

Kerry
WASHINGTON
• • •

As fashionable fixer Olivia Pope on
Scandal, she cleans up political messes in
pantsuits and opera gloves. Offscreen, the
pregnant—and very private—star's style is
more glam than gladiator. "You won't see
me in a power suit," she says. "That's Olivia,
not Kerry." But like her character, the
actress, 36, strays from anything skintight.
"It just doesn't really fit my personality,"
says Washington, who secretly wed NFL pro
Nnamdi Asomugha, 32, this summer. "I'm
not overexposed in my life, and I tend to not
be overexposed on the red carpet."

"It's not dressing
like a nun, and
it's also not
dressing like I'm
in a swimsuit
competition,"
says the star of
her refined style.
"It's finding the
middle ground."

2013 Fashion

Bad
TRENDS

It was a big year
for bottoms,
bra tops and
bewildering
sweatsuits

BRALETTES

• • •

There's a fine
line between
bralettes and
bras. Kat Graham
crossed it.

THE UNDER BUTT

• • •

Stars like Miley Cyrus
sported short shorts that
offered a peek of cheek.

DROP CROTCH

• • •

Brooke Burke-Charvet's harem
pants went to extremes.

HEAD-TO-TOE CAMO

• • •

Kylie Jenner and pals donned matching, army-inspired loungewear—you know, to blend in.

PJS IN PUBLIC

• • •

"You can just mix white trash and Chanel, that's me," Cyrus—boarding a private jet in sleepwear, unicorn slippers and a Chanel bag—told MTV. "That's my ultimate look."

Great Moments in Hair, 2013

At the White House Correspondents' Dinner, the President, during a humorous segment, showed support for his wife's much-discussed new do. Meanwhile, at the Met Ball, Sarah Jessica Parker made waves with history's haute-est mohawk—actually a headress designed by London-based hatmaker Philip Treacy.

09.18.61
06.19.13

James Gandolfini

To his loyal circle of family and friends, Jimmy Gandolfini was a complex, intimidating, big-hearted giant of a man who wryly acknowledged the inevitable comparisons to the Mob boss he embodied for eight seasons on HBO's *The Sopranos*. "I am playing an Italian lunatic from New Jersey, and that's basically what I am," he told *Vogue* in 2001. But after battling his demons through the years—including drug use and a difficult 2002 divorce from Marcy Wudarski, his first wife and mother of their 14-year-old son, Michael—the three-time Emmy winner finally found a hard-won serenity. After the October 2012 birth of daughter Liliana with his wife of four years, former model Deborah Lin, "he was over the moon about being a dad again," says childhood friend Duff Lambros.

But on June 19, Gandolfini died suddenly at age 51 of a heart attack while on vacation in Italy with his son. "When I heard that he was with Michael, I thought, 'At least he was with the great love of his life when he passed,'" says the actor's former fiancée Lora Somoza. "I remember him telling me once, 'The love I have for Michael is primal.' It's a tragedy that his daughter won't know what a great father and a great man he was."

Tributes

Saying farewell to beloved TV legends, the Iron Lady, a thumbs-up film critic, a four-star general, a folkie who accidentally opened Woodstock, and many more

02.29.44

07.22.13

Dennis Farina

He came to his tough-guy roles honestly: For 13 years Dennis Farina was a Chicago cop before a chance meeting with director Michael Mann got him cast as a thug on 1981's *Thief*. The acting bug bit, and Farina continued moonlighting as an actor—including a recurring part as a mobster on *Miami Vice*—but didn't quit the police force until 1985, as he was landing a lead role playing police detective Mike Torello on NBC's *Crime Story*.

As Joe Fontana on *Law & Order* from 2004 to 2006, he personified the dapper NYC detective known for tooling around in a Mercedes and grumbling when crime scenes ruined his Gucci loafers. His craggy mug was tailor-made to play heavies, but he was also a nimble comedian as the f-bombing mobster Ray "Bones" Barboni in *Get Shorty* and in his last TV role, as Nick's charming con-man dad on FOX's *New Girl*.

Farina, who died at 69 in a Scottsdale, Ariz., hospital from a blood clot on his lung, is survived by three sons with his ex-wife Patricia Farina, and by his longtime partner, Marianne Cahill. Called "the pope of old-school Chicago" by Mann, Farina never let Tinseltown get to his head. "Before you actually become an actor," he told the *Newark Star-Ledger,* "maybe there's something to be said for having lived a life."

11.30.75
02.17.13

Mindy McCready

She took Nashville by storm: a record deal at 19, then a double-platinum debut, 1996's *Ten Thousand Angels*, with the No. 1 hit "Guys Do It All the Time." "She didn't sound like anybody else," says producer David Malloy. "She was beautiful but tough."

But the cracks soon began to surface. Fueled by booze and prescription pills, McCready fell into a toxic spiral of domestic violence, suicide attempts, rehab stints and jail time. Her sons, Zander, 7, and Zayne, 1, were at the center of the storm as she publicly battled her mother for custody. Then Zayne's father, songwriter David Wilson, died of an apparently self-inflicted gunshot wound at their Heber Springs, Ark., home. Alone and adrift—her sons had been placed in foster care while she was in rehab—McCready shot herself in the mouth at the very same spot where Wilson had been found. Days before her death, she'd made a suicide prevention video with Danno Hanks—a private investigator she met during a 2010 stint on VH1's *Celebrity Rehab*—that featured the song "I'll See You Yesterday." Says Hanks: "Mindy told me that it was exactly what she wanted." When asked if he could post it, she answered: "You'll know when it's right."

10.22.42
04.08.13

Annette Funicello

To the first wave of kids raised on TV, she was simply Annette—the name emblazoned in block letters across the front of her Mouseketeers turtleneck. On Walt Disney's *The Mickey Mouse Club* from 1955 to 1959 and in 1960s teen film comedies like *Beach Blanket Bingo*, she embodied a dark-eyed, dimpled wholesomeness. As she matured, Funicello left the mouse ears behind, but her fresh-scrubbed sweetness never changed. "Mickey Mouse is my best friend," she said, even as an adult.

On April 8, Funicello succumbed to complications of multiple sclerosis at age 70, with her children Gina, Jack Jr. and Jason Gilardi by her side. "She's on her toes dancing in heaven," said Gina. "No more MS." Forced to retreat from Hollywood, Funicello detailed her health battles in a 1994 autobiography, *A Dream Is a Wish Your Heart Makes*. "By discussing her MS with courage and candor," said Paul Anka, a former boyfriend who wrote his classic song "Puppy Love" about her, "she showed the best side of herself."

In her autobiography, Funicello wrote, "It's funny, but sometimes when I feel discouraged or have a problem I can't work out, I find myself thinking, 'If only Mr. Disney were here, he would know what to do.'"

02.04.23
01.14.13

Conrad Bain

As Phil Drummond, the rich widower who adopts two Harlem kids on *Diff'rent Strokes*, he played the easygoing straight man to Gary Coleman's pint-sized tornado. But Conrad Bain, who had a long career in classical theater, was ever the gentleman, allowing the sitcom's child stars (including Todd Bridges and Dana Plato as his biological daughter) to steal the spotlight. "My father really was a lot like his character," said his daughter Jennifer, who confirmed that her father died of natural causes a few weeks before he turned 90. "He had that warmth and stability." Unfortunately, the "kids" couldn't share his vibe. After the show wrapped in 1986, Plato ran afoul of the law and later committed suicide at age 34; Bridges battled drug addiction for many years; and Coleman, who had medical and financial problems, died at age 42. Bridges told *The Hollywood Reporter* that he considered Bain a real father figure: "Whenever I needed advice, I'd call Conrad," he said. "He was a really good man."

06.18.42
04.04.13

Roger Ebert

On April 3, his 46th anniversary of reviewing movies, Roger Ebert seemed ready for the final credits to roll. The famed critic, 70, continued to write daily throughout his many battles with thyroid and salivary gland cancer—in 2012 he wrote the most reviews of his career—but now the cancer was no longer treatable. "Roger wrote on his notepad, 'Yup, take me home,'" says his stepdaughter Sonia Evans. The next day he gently slipped away, with Chaz—his wife of more than 20 years—by his side.

A Pulitzer Prize–winning critic with the *Chicago Sun-Times*, Ebert became a household name with his spirited thumbs-up-or-down debates with colleague Gene Siskel on *Sneak Previews*, their nationally syndicated TV show. "Few people I've known... cared as much about movies," said director Martin Scorsese. Ebert could be charming ("I was almost hugging myself while I watched it," he wrote of *Almost Famous*) but pulled no punches when he was displeased (of *Crocodile Dundee II*, he said, "I've seen audits that were more thrilling").

His courage and determination in the face of illness is part of his legacy. "It really stinks that the cancer has returned," he wrote in his final blog. "So on bad days I may write about the vulnerability that accompanies illness. On good days, I may wax ecstatic about a movie so good it transports me beyond illness."

01.19.23

05.31.13

Jean Stapleton

As the high-pitched, house-dressed "dingbat" wife of Archie Bunker on *All in the Family,* Stapleton created one of the most beloved characters in television history. At first Stapleton seemed an unlikely candidate for the role. "She was primarily known as a very talented stage actress," says producer Norman Lear. "Even so, I knew she'd be a perfect Edith Bunker." And for nearly a decade (1971-79), she was the bighearted yin to Archie's bigoted, blowhard yang, earning three Emmy Awards and two Golden Globes. In a moving tribute at this year's Emmys, Rob Reiner, who played her *Family* son-in-law, said that "as a performer she was fearless, willing to try anything. Many of Edith's most memorable qualities were inventions of Jean's: her voice, her brilliant comedic timing, her ability to stand up to Archie, and in many scenes, her ability to break your heart."

Stapleton, a lifelong New Yorker, died at home from natural causes at 90. Married to director William Putch for 25 years until his death in 1983, Stapleton had two children who cherish her legacy. "Being the children of a beloved mother on television means sharing the spirit of who Jean Stapleton was," her son and daughter John and Pamela Putch said in a statement. "It is with great love and heavy hearts that we say farewell to our collective Mother with a capital M."

11.08.27
01.01.13

09.12.31
04.26.13

George Jones

"It's a shame to say this, but the booze, the wild life, the women … that's all part of country music," said the legendary George Jones, who put hard living and heartbreak into his songs for more than 50 years. Born near Beaumont, Texas, and discovered by a local record producer, Jones became a hallmark of traditional country music, charting hits in five decades—including 1980's "He Stopped Loving Her Today," often hailed as the best country song ever.

Nicknamed "No Show Jones" for his erratic professional behavior, Jones struggled with cocaine and alcohol addiction in the '70s and early '80s. The father of four also saw three marriages fall apart, including his tortured six years with country icon Tammy Wynette, which begat, among other things, a string of down-home duets unequaled in country music. He got sober in 1984 and turned his life around with help from his fourth wife, Nancy Sepulvado, 64. When he died at 81 of respiratory failure at a Nashville hospital last April, country music knew it had lost "one of the greatest singers in any genre of all time," said country star Kenny Chesney, a friend. "He had a voice that was the truth, raw and unfiltered."

Patti Page

"The Singing Rage, Miss Patti Page" was the Madonna of her day—minus the sex and pyrotechnics. Her 1950s chart toppers "Tennessee Waltz" and "(How Much Is That) Doggie in the Window" spoke of a more wholesome time. "My music was called plastic, antiseptic, placid," she told *The New York Times*—but it sold like hotcakes. Between 1950 and 1965 she scored 24 Top 10 hits and sold 13 million singles. She was the first singer to have TV shows on all three major networks.

Page, who died at 85 in Encinitas, Calif., finally won a Grammy in 1999 for her album *Live at Carnegie Hall: The 50th Anniversary Concert*. She continued to perform into her 80s, never seeming to lose her simple pleasure in singing: "I can tell it all in song: pathos, gladness, love, joy, unhappiness," she told the *Times*. "Each song, you're telling a story."

08.08.21
06.06.13

Esther Williams

She was "America's Mermaid," swimming amid smoke, flame and gushing fountains with a dazzling smile and ne'er a hair out of place. MGM built her a special pool with hydraulic lifts and hidden air hoses where she could perform lavish aquatic choreography in films like 1944's *Bathing Beauty.* After publishing her dishy 1999 memoir, *The Million Dollar Mermaid,* Williams receded from view. But even at 90, a year before she died, she told *Vanity Fair* that her idea of perfect happiness was "a warm sunny day at the pool."

10.20.27
05.13.13

Dr. Joyce Brothers

She was the "mother of mass-media psychology," known for her reassuring advice about sex, relationships and child-rearing. But how many Ph.D.s would show up on *Happy Days* and put Fonzie's depressed dog Spunky on the couch?

Dr. Joyce Brothers was never above poking fun at herself, as she did on shows from *The Love Boat* to *Entourage.* Her five-decade career included movies, radio, newspaper columns and bestselling books, including 1990's *Widowed,* inspired by the death of her husband of 40 years, internist Milton Brothers. Joyce Brothers—who died of respiratory failure at age 85—was, said Dr. Phil McGraw, "a pioneer" who took the mumbo-jumbo out of psychology and gave millions down-to-earth advice they could really use. "Marriage is not just spiritual communion and passionate embraces," she said, but also "remembering to carry out the trash."

04.27.22
12.24.12

Jack Klugman

"I was Oscar Madison," Klugman liked to say about his most famous role, the rumpled, boorish sportswriter in the '70s sitcom *The Odd Couple.* "And the audience loved it." There was plenty to love about the Everyman actor, who spent six decades on stage (playing Herbie in the original 1959 production of *Gypsy*), screen (as Juror No. 5 in the classic *12 Angry Men*) and TV, including *Quincy, M.E.* (1976-1983), playing a crime-solving pathologist.

Klugman, who died at 90 at his Woodland Hills, Calif., home, was slowed in later years by throat cancer. He could only speak in a whisper but doggedly continued to act, regaining enough of his voice to appear in a '91 stage production of *The Odd Couple* opposite his original costar, Tony Randall. The resulting seven-minute standing ovation was, he recalled "the most exciting experience in the world."

11.11.25
04.11.13

Jonathan Winters

An improv genius, Winters was once handed a 3-ft. stick by Jack Paar on the *Tonight Show*, and within four minutes he had channeled 12 characters— including a fisherman, lion tamer, witch, U.N. diplomat and a delusional mental patient who said, "Doctor, I'm not kidding. I've seen them beetles, and this is one of their feelers." As Paar later noted, "If you ask me the funniest 25 people I've ever known, I'd say, 'Here they are—Jonathan Winters.'"

Whether cracking up Johnny Carson as the naughty grandma Maude Frickert or stealing the film from a cast of Hollywood all-stars in 1963's *It's a Mad, Mad, Mad, Mad World*, Winters's zany personae inspired a slew of comedians, including Jim Carrey and Robin Williams. In 1981 he was introduced to a new generation of fans as the son of Williams's alien in the final season of *Mork & Mindy*. "The best stuff was before the cameras were on, when he was open and free to create," Williams said. "Jonathan would just blow the doors off."

Life was not always a madcap frolic. His wife of 60 years, Eileen, said that Winters went through his terrible twos but they lasted 20 years—and at the height of his success, he voluntarily committed himself to a psychiatric hospital. But he kept working, and topped off a six-decade career by voicing Papa Smurf in 2011's *The Smurfs* movie and its 2013 sequel. When he died from natural causes at age 87, Williams paid tribute to his friend and mentor: "He was a rebel without a pause."

01.06.44
03.01.13

Bonnie Franklin

At 5′3″, with a megawatt smile and mop of red hair, Bonnie Franklin looked like the perfect, perky sitcom mom. When she played Ann Romano, a midwestern divorcée struggling to work and raise two teen girls (played by then-newcomers Valerie Bertinelli and Mackenzie Phillips) on *One Day at a Time,* Franklin never wanted to settle for fluff. "Bonnie felt a responsibility to the character and always gave a million notes on the scripts," Phillips wrote in a 2009 memoir. She also pushed to have modern issues, from premarital sex to menopause, addressed at a time when most comedies played it safe. "I am not a director, producer or writer who does his number and then boogies out," she told PEOPLE in 1977. "My face is on the screen and my ass is on the line."

   By putting herself out there as a believable mom on the 1975-1984 CBS sitcom, Franklin, who died of complications of pancreatic cancer at 69, became an inspiration to working mothers—and to Bertinelli, 53, who was just 15 when the show debuted. "She taught me how to navigate this business," said the actress, "and life itself." If her *One Day* legacy also included her distinctive carrot top, Franklin was just fine with that. "I looked like a cocker spaniel," she later joked. "But we weren't doing fashion. We were in Indianapolis!"

10.13.25
04.08.13

Margaret Thatcher

She did not come by her "Iron Lady" sobriquet lightly. Her look (stiff suits, stiffer hair) was daunting, her demeanor imperious, her effect intimidating. That was as she wanted it. "If you just set out to be liked," Margaret Thatcher reflected after 10 years as Britain's prime minister, "you would be prepared to compromise on anything at any time, and you would achieve nothing."

The battles that cemented her reputation as an inflexible conservative—often accomplished hand-in-hand with her friend President Ronald Reagan—were often divisive. Yet during her 11 years at 10 Downing St., beginning in 1979, Thatcher, Europe's first female head of state, also inspired dreams, giving girls around the globe "reason to supplant fantasies of being princesses with a different dream: the real-life option of leading their nation," as Meryl Streep, who portrayed Thatcher in the 2011 film *The Iron Lady*, put it.

After a long battle with dementia, Thatcher, 87, went "peacefully," said her children, twins Mark and Carol, 59, after suffering a stroke on April 8. She was accorded the sort of funeral honors usually reserved for royalty, though she dismissed talk of such pomp as "a waste of money." The 2003 death of her beloved husband, Denis, however, provided a glimpse behind Thatcher's iron facade. "Being prime minister is a lonely job," she said at the time. "But with Denis there, I was never alone."

08.22.34
12.27.12

Norman Schwarzkopf

He led 540,000 U.S. troops into the Persian Gulf in 1991, liberating Kuwait and beating Saddam Hussein's forces into retreat in just six weeks. By the time the dust settled, four-star Army General H. Norman Schwarzkopf, affectionately known as Stormin' Norman, was a household name. He was a new kind of warrior: plainspoken and emotional, and not afraid to ignore the military tradition of tight-jawed stoicism. "He was colorful enough to be really engaging," says Michael O'Hanlon of the Brookings Institution. "He helped keep the country thinking positively about the war."

Schwarzkopf, who died of complications from pneumonia at age 78, was "one of the great military leaders of his generation," President George H.W. Bush, his Gulf War Commander-in-Chief, said in a statement. "He was a good and decent man, and a dear friend." A family man, too. At the 1991 retirement ceremony that capped his 35-year military career, Schwarzkopf cried as he praised his wife, Brenda, and their three children. "They did the most important thing," he said. "When everybody else called me General, you called me Dad."

01.21.41

04.22.13

Richie Havens

If it weren't for the clogged New York State Thruway, Richie Havens might never have become a Woodstock legend. An up-and-coming Greenwich Village folksinger and songwriter, he was slated to play fifth, but the other musicians were stuck in epic traffic jams. Pressed to open the show, he thought, "They're gonna kill me … I need those four people in front of me to warm up the crowd." Going way beyond his allotted time, he sang everything he knew, then began improvising on an old spiritual "Motherless Child," which morphed into his song "Freedom." It electrified the crowd and became an international hit.

Havens, 72, who died of a heart attack at his home in Jersey City, N.J., performed for four more decades, including at President Clinton's first inaugural. But he will forever be associated with the 1969 festival. "It was awesome," he said later, "like double Times Square on New Year's Eve in perfect daylight with no walls or buildings to hold people in place." His ashes were scattered across the farm once owned by Max Yasgur, where Woodstock took place, and where, according to his family, he felt "his deepest connection." "Everything in my life, and so many others," he told the Associated Press in 2009, "is attached to that train."

03.02.42
10.27.13

Lou Reed

He was the '60s antihippie, writing stripped-down songs about New York City's dark corners. In the process Lou Reed, cofounder of the Velvet Underground, became a rock legend who influenced everyone from Nirvana to R.E.M. and U2. As producer Brian Eno noted, if Velvet Underground's debut only sold 30,000 copies, every person "who bought one... started a band."

Reed, who died at 71 from complications of a liver transplant, was the son of a tax accountant and a homemaker who forced him to undergo electroshock therapy to "cure" his supposed bisexuality. After studying literature in college, he moved to New York and jelled with the Velvets; artist Andy Warhol anointed them the house band for his multimedia happenings and produced their first album. In 1970 Reed went solo; the David Bowie-produced single "Walk on the Wild Side" became his only Top 40 hit—with a catchy chorus that belied its depiction of street hustlers and transvestites.

In later years Reed, though always irascible, got sober, married musician Laurie Anderson and took up tai chi. During his 50-year career, he never stopped working and exploring; his last album was a collaboration with Metallica. "People say rock and roll is constricting," he told *The New York Times* in 1982, "but you can do anything you want, any way you want."

Masthead

Editor | Cutler Durkee **Design Director** | Andrea Dunham **Photo Director** | Chris Dougherty **Photo Editor** | C. Tiffany Lee-Ramos **Art Director** | Cynthia Rhett **Writers** | Lisa Russell, Ellen Shapiro, Jill Smolowe, Suzanne Zuckerman **Research** | Hugh McCarten **Copy Editor** | Will Becker **Scanners** | Brien Foy, Salvador Lopez, Stephen Pabarue **Editorial Operations Director** | Richard Prue **Imaging Manager** | Rob Roszkowski **Imaging Production Managers** | Romeo Cifelli, Jeffrey Ingledue

SPECIAL THANKS TO | Céline Wojtala, David Barbee, Jane Bealer, Patricia Clark, Margery Frohlinger, Suzy Im, Ean Sheehy, Patrick Yang

Time Home Entertainment

Publisher | Jim Childs **Vice President, Brand & Digital Strategy** | Steven Sandonato **Executive Director, Marketing Services** | Carol Pittard **Executive Director, Retail & Special Sales** | Tom Mifsud **Executive Publishing Director** | Joy Butts **Director, Bookazine Development & Marketing** | Laura Adam **Finance Director** | Glenn Buonocore **Publishing Director** | Megan Pearlman **Associate General Counsel** | Helen Wan **Assistant Director, Special Sales** | Ilene Schreider **Associate Prepress Manager** | Alex Voznesenskiy **Associate Brand Manager** | Isata Yansaneh **Assistant Production Manager** | Amy Mangus

Editorial Director | Stephen Koepp **Copy Chief** | Rina Bander **Design Manager** | Anne-Michelle Gallero

SPECIAL THANKS: Katherine Barnet, Brad Beatson, Jeremy Biloon, Dana Campolattaro, Susan Chodakiewicz, Rose Cirrincione, Natalie Ebel, Assu Etsubneh, Mariana Evans, Christine Font, Susan Hettleman, Hillary Hirsch, David Kahn, Kimberly Marshall, Nina Mistry, Dave Rozzelle, Ricardo Santiago, Gina Scauzillo, Adriana Tierno, Vanessa Wu

Credits

• • •

FRONT COVER
Clockwise from top: Warner Bros; Optic Photos/Pacific Coast News; Tim Rooke/Rex USA; Miranda Penn Turin/FOX; Theo Wargo/Wireimage; Lionel Hahn/AbacaUSA/Startracks; Michael O'Neill/Corbis Outline

CONTENTS
2 (clockwise from top left) Sean Gallup/Getty Images; Universal Pictures and Illumination Ent.; Joe Buissink; Art Streiber/NBCU; 3 (clockwise from top left) Dario Cantatore/Invision/AP; Splash News; FameFlynet; Jason Bell/Camera Press/Redux

NEWS
4-5 Jason Bell/Camera Press/Redux; 6 (from top) Newspix; Tim Rooke/Rex USA; 7 Peter Nichols/EPA/Landov; 8-9 Jason Bell/Camera Press/Redux; 10 Dan Lampariello/Reuters; (inset) AP; 11 David L. Ryan/The Boston Globe/Getty Images; 12-13 Albert Watson(2); 14 Tim P. Whitby/Getty Images; 15 (from left) Sean Gallup/Getty Images; Optic Photos/PCN; 16 Ramey; 17 Christopher Polk/Getty Images; 18 Wilford Harewood/NBCU/Getty Images; 19 Lou Rocco/ABC/Getty Images; 20-21 Art Streiber/NBCU; 22-23 (clockwise from left) Craig Harris/Wenn; WeirPhotos/Splash News; FameFlynet; Maciel-Twist-WL/X 17; Raef-Ramirez/AKM-GSI; FameFlynet; Breedo/Splash News; 247PapsTV/Splash News; 24-25 (from left) Courtesy Kim Kardashian & Kanye West; Albert Michael/Startraks; Ewen MacAskill/The Guardian/Reuters; 26 Theo Wargo/Wireimage; 27 (from top) Elvina Beck/RCA; Joe Burbank/The New York Times/Redux; 28-29 Nick Oxford/The New York Times/Redux; 30-31 (from left) Alexandra Wyman/Getty Images; Bauer-Griffin; PGP/Newspics/Abaca USA(2); 32-33 (clockwise from left) Brigitte Stelzer/Splash News; Hennes Paynter Communications/Xposure(3); Scott Shaw/The Plain Dealer/Landov; Marvin Fong/The Plain Dealer/Landov; Roadell Hickman; 34 Todd Rosenberg/Sports Illustrated/Getty Images; (inset) Peter Kramer/NBC NewsWire/Getty Images; 35 (clockwise from top) Splash News; Pierre-Philippe Marcou/AFP/Getty Images; Paul Harris/PCN; Bob D'Amico/Getty Images

CRIME
36 James Glossop/The Times Glasgow/NI Syndication; 37 (from top) Siphiwe Sibeko/Reuters/Landov; Reuters; 38-39 (clockwise from left) Elder Ordonez/INF; Bob Gay/The Dominion Post/AP; Courtesy Neese Family; Dave Kotinsky/Getty Images; 40 (from left) Chicago Tribune/MCT/Landov; Courtesy of Family of Stacy Peterson/AP; 41 (artwork) Courtesy Police Rotterdam/AP(2); (frames) Yuri Arcurs/Alamy

GALLERY
42-43 Juan Oliphant(2); 44 Gade/AKM-GSI; 45 Kevin Mazur/Wireimage; 46-47 Caters News Agency; 48 (from top) MediaPunch/Face to Face; MiamiPixx/FameFlynet; 49 Earl Gibson III/Wireimage(2); 50-51 Brian Doben

WEDDINGS
52-53 Amelia J. Moore(2); 54 Spread/X 17; 55 Brian Leahy(2); 56 Meg Smith; 57 Tyrone Siu/Reuters/Landov; 58 Caitlin Maloney Photography; 59 Courtesy Melissa Gilbert & Timothy Busfield; 60 Jonathan Leibson/Wireimage; 61 Koby & Terilyn Brown/Archetype Studio Inc.; 62 Joe Buissink; 63 Mark Seliger; 64 Kevin Winter/Getty Images; 65 Mike Larson/Getty Images; 66 Hello! 2013 ©/Florian Kalotay; 67 Mark Liddell

ENGAGED
68-69 Kwaku Alston/Corbis Outline; 70 Kevin Mazur/Wireimage; 71 Christopher Polk/Wireimage; 72 Francisco Roman/ABC; 73 Jerod Harris/Wireimage; 74 Frank Trapper/Corbis; 75 Courtesy Tiger Woods & Lindsey Vonn

SPLITS
76 Eric Charbonneau/Wireimage; 77 Splash News/Corbis; 78 Charley Gallay/Getty Images; 79 Chris Ashford/Camera Press/Redux; 80 Dimitrios Kambouris/Wireimage; 81 Jim Ruymen/UPI/Landov; 82 Axelle Woussen/Bauer Griffin; 83 (from top) Sara De Boer/Startraks; Bruce Glikas/Filmmagic

BABIES
84-85 Chris Knight(2); 86 Courtesy Channing Tatum; 87 (from top) Alison Dyer; Courtesy Jenna Bush Hager

MOVIES
88-89 Disney; (insets from top) Zade Rosenthal/Disney; Universal Pictures & Illumination Entertainment; 90-91 (clockwise from top left) Jaap Buitendijk/Paramount; Warner Bros; Zade Rosenthal/Paramount; Film District; Reiner Bajo/Sony Pictures Ent.; Warner Bros.; Jessica Miglio/ Sony Pictures Classics

TV
92-93 Art Streiber/A&E; 94 (from top) Frank Ockenfels/AMC; Eric Liebowitz/NBC; 95 (clockwise from top left) Rodolfo Martinez/NBCU/Getty Images; Kelsey MCneal/ Getty Images; Cliff Lipson/CBS/Landov; Helen Sloan/HBO

MUSIC
96-97 Mark Davis/Getty Images; (insets from left) Gary Gershoff/Wireimage; Inez & Vinoodh/42 West; 98 (from top) Frank Hoensch/Redferns/Getty Images; Shirlaine Forrest/Wireimage; Kevin Mazur/Wireimage; 99 FameFlynet

FASHION
100-101 Matt Sayles/Invision/AP; 102-103 (from left) FameFlynet; Lionel Hahn/AbacaUSA/Startraks; Jeff Kravitz/Getty Images; Fernando Allende/Broadimage; Jason Merritt/Getty Images; Evan Agostini/Invision/AP; 104-105 (from left) Briquet-Hahn-Marechal/Abaca/Startracks; Matt Baron/BEImages; Rachel Kelly/Photo Image Press; Christopher Polk/Getty Images; David Hitchens/Capital Pictures/Retna; Dennis Van Tine/Future Image/Wenn; 106 (from left) Pascal Le Segretain/Getty Images; DLM Press/PCN; INF; Jon Kopaloff/Filmmagic; 107 (clockwise from left) Can Nguyen/AdMedia; Broadimage; Joe Schildhorn/BFAnyc/Sipa USA; Jason Merritt/Getty Images; Dario Cantatore/Invision/AP; Steve Granitz/Wireimage; 108 (from left) Pacific Coast News; Tony DiMaio/Startracks; VM-Dino/FameFlynet; 109 (clockwise from bottom right) Fairchld Photo Service/Newscom; Luca Chelsea/Splash; AKM-GSI

TRIBUTES
110-111 Michael O'Neill/Corbis Outline; 112 Will Hart/NBCU/Getty Images; 113 Daniela Stallinger/Corbis Outline; 114 Tom Kelley/MPTV; 115 Everett; 116 Joseph Cultice/Corbis Outline; 117 MPTV; 118 Hulton Archive/Getty Images; 119 Michael Ochs Archives/Getty Images; 120 MPTV; 121 (from left) Ann Clifford/DMI/Time Life Pictures/Getty Images; ABC Photo Archives/Getty Images; 122 Gabi Rona/MPTV; 123 Steve Schapiro; 124 Nigel Parry/CPI; 125 David Turnley/Corbis; 126 Steph/Visual/Zuma; 127 Steven Dewall/Retna; 128 Jason Bell/Camera Press/Redux

BACK COVER
Clockwise from top left: Art Streiber/NBCU; Fairchld Photo Service/Newscom; GADE/AKM-GSI; Wilford Harewood/NBCU/Getty Images; Jim Fiscus/AETN; Courtesy Tiger Woods/Lindsey Vonn; Eric Charbonneau/Wireimage; Universal Pictures & Illumination Entertainment